Drawing Connections

Drawing Connections

Baselitz, Kelly, Penone, Rockburne, and the Old Masters

Isabelle Dervaux

FOREWORD BY
Charles E. Pierce, Jr.

THE MORGAN LIBRARY & MUSEUM, NEW YORK

Exhibition at The Morgan Library & Museum, 12 October 2007–6 January 2008

Major support for *Drawing Connections: Baselitz, Kelly, Penone, Rockburne, and the Old Masters* was provided by the Lily Auchincloss Foundation, Inc.

Additional support for this publication and related programs was provided by Jan Abrams Fine Arts; the Herman Goldman Foundation; Marian Goodman Gallery, New York; Greenberg Van Doren Gallery, New York; Matthew Marks Gallery; Kathleen O'Grady; Michael and Juliet Rubenstein; and Teresa Liszka and Martin Weinstein.

Library of Congress Cataloging-in-Publication Data

Dervaux, Isabelle.
  Drawing connections : Baselitz, Kelly, Penone, Rockburne, and the old masters / Isabelle Dervaux ; foreword by Charles E. Pierce, Jr.
      p. cm.
  Catalog of an exhibition at the Morgan Library & Museum, Oct. 12, 2007-Jan. 6, 2008.
  Includes bibliographical references.
  ISBN 978-0-87598-147-5 (alk. paper)
  1. Drawing, European--Exhibitions. 2. Drawing--20th century—Exhibitions. 3. Baselitz, Georg, 1938—Exhibitions. 4. Kelly, Ellsworth, 1923—Exhibitions. 5. Penone, Giuseppe—Exhibitions. 6. Rockburne, Dorothea—Exhibitions. I. Pierpont Morgan Library. II. Title.

  NC225.D466 2007
  741.9074'7471--dc22

2007026955

ISBN: 978-0-87598-147-5

Published by The Morgan Library & Museum
Karen Banks, Publications Manager
Patricia Emerson, Senior Editor
Elizabeth Moore, Editorial Assistant

Project staff
Marilyn Palmeri, Manager, Photography and Rights

Designed by Katy Homans
Printed and bound by Meridian Printing, East Greenwich, RI

FRONT COVER: Giuseppe Penone, *The Imprint of Drawing, Right Ring Finger,* 2001 (detail)
© 2007 Artists Rights Society (ARS), New York / ADAGP, Paris

BACK COVER: Domenico Beccafumi, *Head of an Old Man with Open Mouth,* ca. 1529–35

Printed in the United States of America

Table of Contents

Director's Foreword

Almost ten years ago, The Morgan Library & Museum decided to expand the chronological range of its drawings collection to include twentieth-century art. At the same time, it embarked on a program of exhibitions devoted to modern and contemporary drawings. These have included *New York Collects: Drawings and Watercolors, 1900–1950; Stuart Davis: Art and Theory, 1920–31; Saul Steinberg: Illuminations;* and *From Berlin to Broadway: The Ebb Bequest of Modern German and Austrian Drawings. Drawing Connections* proposes to explore the interaction between contemporary and old master drawings by juxtaposing works created centuries apart. To this end, four artists—Georg Baselitz, Ellsworth Kelly, Giuseppe Penone, and Dorothea Rockburne—were invited to select works from the Morgan's collection. Their selection is exhibited next to some of their own drawings. The ensuing visual dialogue makes it apparent that the relationship between contemporary art and that of the past is a two-way street. If the artists' selections of old master works reveal many insights into their own works, at the same time their drawings bring new perspectives to bear on the Morgan's collection of old master drawings.

With its extraordinary holdings of over ten thousand sheets from the fifteenth to nineteenth centuries, the Morgan is in a unique position to offer such a reflection on draftsmanship through the centuries. Contemporary and old master drawings seem to be poles apart—in terms of style, size, materials and techniques, and often function—yet because of the immediacy of the medium, recent drawings are comparable to those of the past in that they provide a better understanding of an artist's intentions and illuminate the workings of the creative mind.

I extend my profound gratitude to the artists who have responded with enthusiasm to our invitation to participate in this exhibition and have given some of their precious time to make this new venture in the history of the Morgan a success. I also thank Isabelle Dervaux, curator of modern and contemporary drawings, for conceiving this exhibition and working closely with each artist to organize it.

For its financial support of the exhibition, I would like to thank the Lily Auchincloss Foundation, Inc. The production of this catalogue was supported by generous contributions from Jan Abrams, the Herman Goldman Foundation, Marian Goodman Gallery, Greenberg Van Doren Gallery, Matthew Marks Gallery, Kathleen O'Grady, Michael and Juliet Rubenstein, and Teresa Liszka and Martin Weinstein. To all of them I extend my warmest thanks.

Charles E. Pierce, Jr.

Acknowledgments

Heartfelt thanks are due first to Georg Baselitz, Ellsworth Kelly, Giuseppe Penone, and Dorothea Rockburne, who have participated in this exhibition, taking the time to select old master drawings, lending several of their own works, and contributing statements to this catalogue. It was a memorable experience to look at drawings with them in the storage vault at the Morgan. I am also most grateful to the other lenders, namely, Carol Eckman and David Nolan, Marian Goodman, Michael Werner, and private collectors who wish to remain anonymous. The artists' assistants—Detlev Gretenkort in Georg Baselitz's studio; Sandi Knakal, Mark Moffett, and Eva Walters in Ellsworth Kelly's studio; Thomas Martin, Jinnine Pac, and Ben La Rocco in Dorothea Rockburne's studio—have kindly and tirelessly answered numerous requests. Ruggero Penone graciously supplied photography of his father's work.

At the galleries that represent these artists, I am thankful to Sarah Fritchey and David Nolan at David Nolan Gallery, Marian Goodman and Leslie Nolen at Marian Goodman Gallery, and Gordon Veneklasen and Jason Duval at Michael Werner Gallery. At the Morgan, many people have assisted in different facets of this exhibition and catalogue, and I am most appreciative of their help: Robert Parks, director of library and museum services; Rhoda Eitel-Porter, Jennifer Tonkovich, Kathleen Stuart, Andaleeb Banta, Justine Pokoik, Vanessa Aubry, and Matthias Koddenberg in the Drawings and Prints department; Margaret Holben Ellis, Patricia Reyes, and James Donchez in the Thaw Conservation Center; Marilyn Palmeri, Joseph Zehavi, and Alessandra Merrill in the Photography and Rights department; John Alexander, Patricia Courtney, and Sloane Whidden in the Registrar's office; and Karen Banks, Patricia Emerson, and Elizabeth Moore in the Publications department. Michael Rubenstein deserves special thanks for his help in raising funds to produce this catalogue, which was superbly designed by Katy Homans.

Introduction

The contrast between the rarefied world of old master drawings and the effervescent contemporary art scene is such that one would expect few connections between them. Drawings today come in a wide range of sizes, materials, and techniques, sometimes far removed from traditional ones. No longer related to painting and sculpture, drawing has achieved a more independent status in the twentieth century. Its very definition has been questioned as the term has evolved to encompass a broad variety of works—think of Sol LeWitt's wall drawings.

And yet many contemporary artists whose work appears to have nothing in common with old master drawings are fascinated by them. This exhibition proposes to bridge centuries and engage a reflection on the art of drawing by bringing together old masters and contemporary works. Four artists have been invited to select a few sheets from the Morgan's renowned collection of old master drawings to be exhibited next to some of their own work. From such a compare-and-contrast exercise, unexpected connections emerge between past and present, showing not only what contemporary art owes to the art of the past but also how our interpretation of earlier art is indebted to contemporary practices.

The artists invited to take part in this project—Georg Baselitz, Ellsworth Kelly, Giuseppe Penone, and Dorothea Rockburne—represent radically divergent artistic directions. They have in common, however, the centrality of the medium of drawing to their work along with a profound interest in the art of the past. All four responded enthusiastically to this unique opportunity to confront their drawings directly with those of some of the greatest masters. Each artist was given carte blanche to select works from the Morgan's collection according to his or her personal criteria, a task that each approached differently. [1]

Baselitz, without hesitation, chose the Florentine mannerists. Excited to learn that the Morgan counted no fewer than forty drawings by Parmigianino, he decided to focus on this artist. His decision was not surprising. Since the early 1960s, especially after a six-month fellowship at the Villa Romana in Florence in 1965, Baselitz has had a passionate interest in the works of Parmigianino, Pontormo, Rosso, and other sixteenth-century Italian artists. Their anticlassical stance and nonacademic approach echoed his own rejection of artistic conventions. He began collecting their prints and now owns over 250 of them. "Through some of these prints," he wrote, "I have been able to underscore my own vision and my theories. . . . For there was in them a freedom almost revolutionary in comparison to Germany." [2] The German tradition that Baselitz rejected was that of Dürer, whom he finds boring. "What interests me in art are these borderline cases when the knowledge that has been acquired becomes uncertain and the classical image begins to unravel. From that point on, everything becomes more lively. . . . The imagination is more unbound than the tape measurer." [3] The mannerists' disregard for classical canons of representation, which led them to draw figures of exaggerated proportions and in unlikely poses, corresponded to Baselitz's own approach. In the early 1960s, he depicted distorted and grotesque bodies (see p. 16). Under the influence of mannerism, he adopted a freer and more sensuous style in which figures emerge from a rich network of curved lines (p. 17). Inspired by the mannerists' emphasis on the aesthetic effect for its own sake, Baselitz rejected the symbolist iconography of his earlier works and developed a series of formal strategies to call attention to the properties of painting or drawing themselves. This led first to the "fracture" paintings and drawings, in which the surface is broken up in several sections that dislocate the image (pp. 19–20). In turn this dislocation opened the way, in 1969, to the reversal of the image, a device that allowed him, in his own words, "to liberate representation from content," and has remained a hallmark of his style (p. 21).[4] John Shearman's description of Italian mannerism also summarizes Baselitz's achievements. "What the work stimulates positively is not belief in a narrative, not the evocation of something real outside itself, but fascination in itself, in its complexities, its visual jokes, its *tours de force* of manipulation and technique, and its accumulated demonstration of artistic capacity."[5]

It may seem initially puzzling that two artists as different from each other as Baselitz and Rockburne have both chosen to exhibit sixteenth-century Italian drawings. Rockburne's passion for the art of the past has been essential to her own work from the beginning of her career. Her wide-ranging interests include, among others, Greek and Incan architecture, Egyptian wall reliefs, early Italian Renaissance painting, mannerism, and van Gogh. She feels a profound link with her predecessors. "Studying art history to a point of deep, personal understanding allowed me to feel a remarkably human connection to all people through time," she said.[6] If Baselitz was attracted to mannerist artists for their excesses and freedom from the classical tradition, Rockburne is fascinated by their strange use of perspective and complex spatial structures. The poses and gestures of the figures in a Pontormo or Tintoretto defy the laws of perspective as they were established in the fifteenth century. The spatial complexity of mannerism resonates with Rockburne's interest in physics and the visualization of scientific concepts. Among other pursuits, she has given considerable attention to the study of perspective. One reason for her admiration for the mannerists, she explained, is that they "began to change perspectival things around in quite a radical way."[7] The contortions of the figures in a mannerist work lead the eye through the space of the picture itself, creating a spatial construction independent from reality. Rockburne describes mannerist space as "kind of voluminous. It's always kind of going up, up, and things get congested, and there is no exact vanishing point. However, it is not a flat space."[8] Exploring the idea of a different kind of perspective in her own work as well, in the early 1970s Rockburne conceived several series of drawings made by folding paper according to mathematical rules so that each work generates itself in the process. On the surface the visual restraint and quietness of these works, such as the *Conservation Class* series (pp. 40 – 41), seem poles apart from the mannerist excesses, but their structural complexity and the way in which they create their own space are indeed similar. Several of the Italian drawings that Rockburne selected in the Morgan's collection are details of figures, chiefly heads and hands. These powerful close-ups constitute a concentrated version of the complex spatial effects of more elaborate, multifigure compositions. The torsion of a head (p. 45) or the simple twist of a hand (p. 42) suggest a whole space swirling around them.

Rockburne also credited mannerism as a source for her more recent work based on astronomy. "I think perhaps it was the perspective used in Mannerism, and carried on in late van Goghs that visually led me into astronomy," she said.[9] From her reading of scientific treatises, combined with her own observations, during the last two decades Rockburne has created colorful and luminous paintings on paper conjuring up her vision of the cosmos (pp. 38 and 44). Although color and light have always been important in her work, the glowing palette of the astronomy drawings has brought forth the synthesis of intellectual complexity and emotion that is the basis of her art, and that also links her to her mannerist forebears.

Unlike Baselitz and Rockburne, Ellsworth Kelly did not focus on one particular school or period in his selection. The works he chose are relatively modern, from the seventeenth to the twentieth century and primarily by artists from the north—Lucas Achtschellinck, a seventeenth-century Flemish landscape painter known for his forest scenes; Rubens; van Gogh; and two artists from northern France, Watteau and Matisse. Ingres and Degas complete this predominantly French selection, perhaps a reflection of Kelly's love for the country where he lived from 1948 to 1954. But it was not so much the artists as the specific drawings that guided Kelly's choice. In perusing the drawings in the Morgan's storage room, he was attracted to details, pointing to the movement of a line or the economy of a form suggested by a few rapid strokes. Such attention to detail is reminiscent of Kelly's working method, which consists in selecting fragments of the world around him—an architectural detail, the contour of a shadow—and using them as inspiration for his abstract paintings.

Not surprisingly, the common denominator of the sheets Kelly picked is their linear quality—a characteristic that relates them to his own practice. In his graphic production, Kelly has always favored contour drawings, with little or no shading or modeling. Best known among these are his plant drawings made from observation. Depicting plant leaves devoid of context, these drawings are exercises in pure two-dimensional forms (p. 26). "The plant drawings," Kelly explained, "are exact observations of the form of the leaf of flower or fruit seen. Nothing is changed or added: no shading, no surface marking. They are not an approximation of the thing seen, nor are they a personal expression or an abstraction. They are an impersonal observation of the form."[10] Among the Morgan's sheets that Kelly selected only Matisse's *Self-Portrait* (p. 29) is a contour drawing, but in all of them line plays a dominant role in the construction of the image. Watteau's *Study of a Young Man* (p. 22) and, especially, van Gogh's *Wheat Field* (p. 26) are built from an amazing variety of strokes that not only generate the image but also give it its wonderful rhythm.

Another characteristic of Kelly's selection of old master drawings is that several of them are preparatory sketches. They have this unfinished quality that calls attention to the act of drawing itself by exposing the artist's method and process—a feature particularly appealing to an artist. In some of the drawings (Watteau and Ingres, pp. 22 and 25), the presence on the same sheet of fragments of figures on different scales produces spatial disjunctions and unexpected juxtapositions, making them appear so modern to the eye trained through cubism and surrealism.

But perhaps what best unifies Kelly's selection and most directly relates it to his own work is the economy of means that all of these drawings share. Nothing superfluous on these sheets—each line has a specific function in the making of the image. Although the drawings depict figures or landscapes, they have a high degree of abstraction. Rather than trying to create the illusion of a reality outside of the drawing, they bring home the process of transformation by which a few lines become an expressive image. Degas's *Standing Man in a Bowler Hat* (p. 27) is remarkable in this regard: a few bold strokes of the brush delineate the figure in contrast with the more precisely drawn face suggesting the man's psychological state. There is a directness and sense of efficiency in this drawing comparable to Kelly's own approach, as can be seen in his portrait of his dead brother, *Allan Kelly, Sr. (After Death;* p. 27).

Giuseppe Penone's work deals with man's relation to nature, not just through observation but in a more intimate fashion, through all the senses, particularly touch. His drawings, like his sculptures, are often produced through direct contact between the artist's body and a support. They reflect a very sensual approach to the artistic process and to the world in general. In looking at old master drawings, Penone was less concerned with technique or style than with the "vision of reality" that the act of drawing itself reflected (see p. 30). He proposed three groups of drawings that correspond, in his view, to three different types of relationship between man and his surrounding world, with each group bearing a relationship to one aspect of Penone's own work. The groups cut across geographical and chronological borders to bring together works that have a deeper connection in their visualization of a particular outlook. This can be expressed in the subject but also comes through in the artist's choice of technique, material, and process.

In the first group, Penone relates José de Ribera's *Marsyas Bound to a Tree,* a monumental prison interior by Piranesi, and the broad vista of a mountain landscape attributed to Bruegel to his own 1968 studies for his intervention on the growth of trees (pp. 32–33). To him, all of these represent the domination of man by his environment. The myth of Marsyas—who, after he lost a contest with Apollo, was bound to a tree and flayed—is particularly relevant to Penone because of the presence of the tree. Ribera's drawing emphasizes the anthropomorphism of the tree to which Marsyas is bound, with its two branches extending like arms on either side of the trunk. Such a correspondence between the human body and a tree is central to Penone, who has based many sculptures on it, and whose dream of fusion between human and vegetal is given visual form in his drawing of a tree trunk growing around and enveloping a head (p. 33).[11]

The drawings of the second group feature a highly precise technique put to the service of an objective rendering of the world. The artist's mastery in his total control of the medium is manifest in the precision of the final image, achieved through a labor-intensive process. The works of Dürer and Mantegna exemplify such extraordinary draftsmanship developed with the purpose of representing the real world with the greatest accuracy (pp. 30 and 34). One of Penone's own drawings in this group, *The Imprint of Drawing* (p. 35), is an astonishing amplification of one of his fingerprints by means of freely drawn concentric circles, one millimeter apart from each other, on a six-by-four-foot sheet of paper. As the lines engendered by the fingerprint design evolve into the growth rings of some ancient tree, the drawing becomes a powerful visualization of the creative power of man fusing with that of nature.

The third group of drawings selected by Penone—a Bernini portrait, a watercolor landscape by Cézanne, and a nude by Klimt—takes the opposite stance. Instead of maintaining such tight control over his material, the artist "abandons himself" to it, as Penone describes it. As a result, a sense of freedom emerges from these works, from their unfinished quality, their flowing rhythm, the unexpected reaction of their support to the medium. From this spontaneity and fluidity the sensuality of nature comes through. "There exists an ensemble of values, sensations, knowledge, emotions, and perceptions related to matter itself that a mathematical reading of reality will never give us: it is sensuality," Penone wrote in a text about the fundamental role of the senses in art.[12]

The connections that Penone established between the drawings he selected disregard traditional forms of categorization in favor of an idiosyncratic vision of art history inspired by the artist's own practice. In identifying points of contact between seemingly very different works, Penone illuminates his own art while renewing our appreciation of familiar images by showing them from a different perspective.

In recent years, a few museums have invited artists to curate exhibitions or have commissioned them to create works based on their collection. *Encounters, Counterpoint, Correspondences,* and *Uninterrupted Dialogue* are the titles of some of these exhibitions that underscore the continuity between the art of the past and that of our time.[13] In comparison to these initiatives, *Drawing Connections* is a more focused exhibition specifically addressing the history of drawing as a medium. It does not so much aim at revealing influences, allusions, or references but at exploring more fundamental correspondences by taking a broader view of drawing as the medium closest to the artist's mental processes. The artist Sigmar Polke described his drawings as "things I make for myself . . . mental experiments—private inner thoughts."[14] Selected by artists, the old master drawings in this exhibition are presented outside their historical context. They have been chosen for their significance in relation to living art, in a dialogue between past and present engaged in by artists who are making their own contribution to the history of drawing. Artists are connected across boundaries of style and epochs, through a kinship that the British painter Walter Sickert expressed forcefully: "And this, gentlemen of the press, curators, critics, experts and others, is the claim we painters make in regard to the old masters. They are ours, not yours. We have their blood in our veins."[15] In following the lead of the artists who have selected the works for this exhibition, and in looking at drawings through their eyes, perhaps we will become privy to some of the family secrets.

1. The only restriction was that some drawings were already promised for loans or that some, having been exhibited recently, couldn't be shown again because of their sensitivity to light.

2. Quoted in *La bella maniera: La collection d'estampes maniéristes de Georg Baselitz,* École nationale supérieure des beaux-arts, Paris 2002, p. 13.

3. *Le beau style, 1520–1620: Gravures maniéristes de la collection Georg Baselitz,* Cabinet des estampes, Geneva, 2002, p. 11.

4. Quoted in Diane Waldman, *Georg Baselitz,* Guggenheim Museum, New York 1995, p. 71.

5. John Shearman, *Mannerism,* Harmonsworth, England 1967, p. 68.

6. Transcript of a lecture delivered at Princeton University, September 28, 2004, pp. 8–9. I am grateful to Dorothea Rockburne for making this transcript available to me.

7. Ibid., pp. 30–31.

8. Quoted in Michael Brenson, "The Artist's Eye: Dorothea Rockburne. A New-World Painter Views the Masterpieces of Old-World Innovators," *The New York Times,* 29 April 1988, p. C36.

9. E-mail from Dorothea Rockburne to David Reed, 29 November 2006. My thanks to

Dorothea Rockburne for sharing this correspondence with me.

10. "Notes from 1969," in *Ellsworth Kelly: Paintings and Sculptures, 1963–1979,* Barbara Rose, ed., Stedelijk Museum, Amsterdam 1979–80, p. 33.

11. In a text written in 1986, Penone described tree branches as "so intimately human." Giuseppe Penone, *Respirer l'ombre,* Paris 1999, p. 141.

12. Ibid., p. 140.

13. These were held primarily in Europe. *Correspondences* and *Counterpoint* are the generic titles of series of exhibitions held respectively at the Musée d'Orsay and the Louvre in the last few years, for which artists are commissioned to create works in relation to works in the collections of these museums. For the full citations of the other exhibitions mentioned here, see the Selected Bibliography.

14. Quoted in Carol Vogel, "The Alchemist's Moment," *The New York Times,* 27 May 2007, section 2, p. 20.

15. Quoted in David Cohen, "Artists at an Exhibition," *The New York Times Book Review,* 4 October 1998, p. BR38.

Georg Baselitz

Parmigianino

Perhaps because around 1964 I was somewhat unhappy with the Gothic stiffness of the German school, I was enthusiastic about Parmigianino, the Italian mannerist, whom I had discovered in Gustav René Hocke's book, *Die Welt als Labyrinth* (The World as a Labyrinth). I wanted to have what was so foreign to me, what I did not have myself, and I wanted to incorporate it. Parmigianino is grace, more than manner and style, he is sensuousness and grace.

His beginning with Raphael, his enormous talent, the small number of his paintings and drawings, his fifteen prints, and yet his large circle of admirers, followers, and imitators — that attracted me, that was so far removed from me and from what I was doing (at that time, the feet, for instance), but that is what I wanted to have, that was my dream.

Munich, December 10, 2006

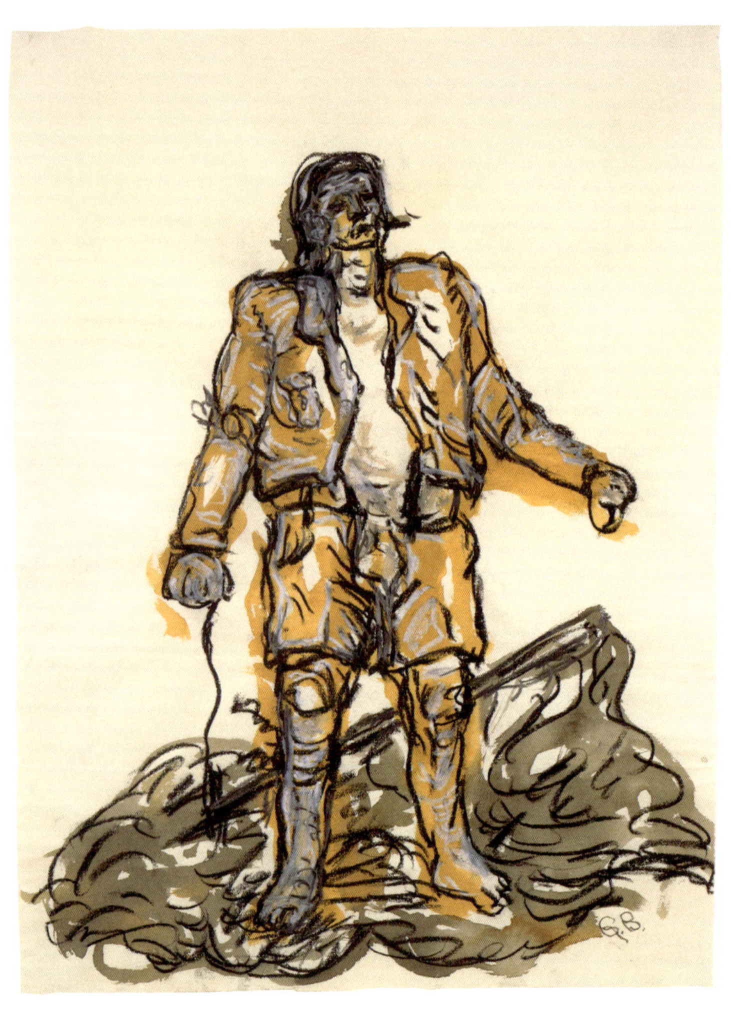

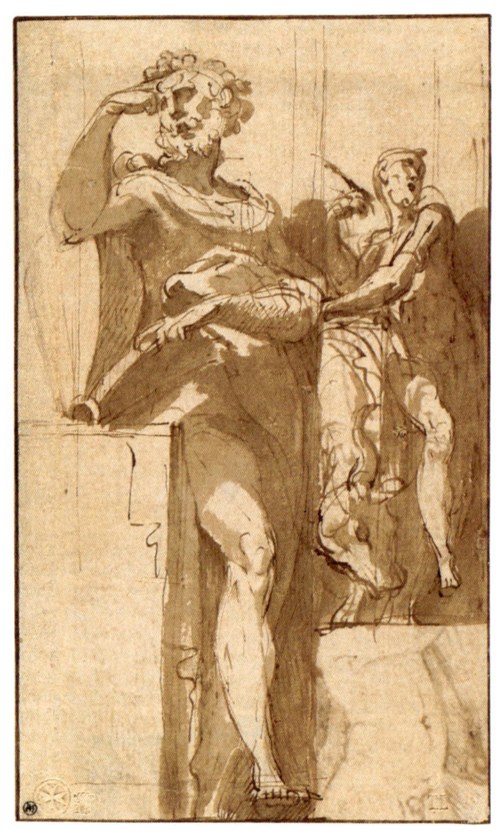

Georg Baselitz, *A New Type*, 1965

Parmigianino, *Man Standing Beside a Plinth on Which He Rests a Book*, 1530s

Georg Baselitz was born Georg Kern in 1938 in Deutschbaselitz, Saxony. Raised near Dresden, he moved to East Berlin in 1956 to enroll at the Hochschule für Bildende Künste, from which he was soon expelled for "sociopolitical immaturity." He continued his artistic training in West Berlin while immersing himself in the writings of Nietzsche, Baudelaire, Lautréamont, and Artaud, all of whom exerted a strong influence on him. Reacting against the abstract tendencies that dominated West German art of the fifties, Baselitz adopted an expressive figurative idiom marked by a crude handling and grotesque, often sexual, imagery. His paintings caused a scandal during his first solo exhibition at the Galerie Werner & Katz in Berlin in 1963, and two of them were confiscated by the public prosecutor for obscenity.

In 1965, during a six-month fellowship in Florence, Baselitz developed an interest in sixteenth-century Italian mannerism, the anti-classical stance of which appealed to him. The odd proportions and exaggerated poses typical of mannerist figures soon found their way into his work, notably his series of Heroes and his so-called fracture paintings of 1967–69. In the latter Baselitz fragmented the image and divided the picture plane into several sections in order to play down the narrative implications of the painting and draw attention instead to its pictorial qualities. The same concern led him, in 1969, to invert his motifs, a device that would become the hallmark of his style and liberated him from the dilemma between figuration and abstraction.

Concurrently with his paintings, Baselitz produced a large body of drawings in which he explored the same themes and compositional strategies. His formless and often gruesome images of the early 1960s gave way after 1965 to figures drawn more freely with a multiplicity of curved lines, influenced by the mannerist prints that the artist had begun collecting. Working in series—another way to deemphasize the importance of the subject in favor of its formal treatment—Baselitz developed a more abstract imagery in the following decades. In the 1990s, his painting style became looser and more fluid, in parallel with his abundant production of watercolors. Baselitz's urge to revisit earlier motifs culminated in his recent Remix series, a large group of paintings and drawings in which he has been reworking themes and compositions from earlier pictures.

Selection of Old Master Drawings

Parmigianino
(Italian, 1503–1540)

The Virgin Seated with Yarn Winder, and the Infant Christ Embracing the Infant St. John, early 1520s
Red chalk on paper; framing line along lower edge in pen and brown ink
8¼ x 6 inches (209 x 151 mm)
Gift of J. P. Morgan, Jr., 1924; IV, 40

Girl Seated on the Ground Near a Chair, ca. 1524
Pen and brown ink, brown wash on paper
5⅞ x 5³⁄₁₆ inches (136 x 131 mm)
Gift of J. P. Morgan, Jr., 1924; IV, 46a

Prometheus Animating Man, ca. 1524–27
Pen and brown ink, brown wash, over black chalk on paper
5⅜ x 6¹⁄₁₆ inches (135 x 154 mm)
Gift of J. P. Morgan, Jr., 1924; IV, 45

Study of Figures in the Foreground of the Marriage of the Virgin, ca. 1526
Red chalk, pen and brown ink, light brown wash on paper
7 x 9⅛ inches (179 x 231 mm)
Gift of J. P. Morgan, Jr., 1924; I, 48

Virgin and Child with the Infant St. John the Baptist, ca. 1527–31
Black chalk, brown wash on paper
4¹³⁄₁₆ x 3⅞ inches (122 x 95 mm)
Gift of J. P. Morgan, Jr., 1924; IV, 48

Man Standing Beside a Plinth on Which He Rests a Book, and a Smaller Study of a Standing Man with Ox, 1530s
Pen and brown ink, brown wash, over traces of black chalk or graphite on paper
6½ x 3¹⁵⁄₁₆ inches (164 x 99 mm)
Gift of J. P. Morgan, Jr., 1924; I, 46c

Attributed to Parmigianino

Death Appearing to Three Philosophers, ca. 1520–24
Red chalk on paper
6 x 6¾ inches (152 x 172 mm)
Gift of Janos Scholz; 1989.66

Drawings by Georg Baselitz

The Whip Woman (Die Peitschenfrau), 1964
Watercolor, charcoal, chalk on paper
25 x 19¼ inches (635 x 489 mm)
Private collection

A New Type (Ein neuer Typ), 1965
Gouache, pastel, oil stick, graphite on handmade paper
19⅝ x 15 inches (500 x 380 mm)
Courtesy Michael Werner Gallery, New York and Cologne

Kullervo, or Dog Boy, 1966/67
Watercolor, pencil, charcoal on paper
17 x 12 inches (432 x 305 mm)
Private collection

Divided Hero, 1966/67
Charcoal and wash on paper
24 x 17 inches (610 x 432 mm)
Collection of David Nolan and Carol Eckman, New York

Untitled, 1966/67
India ink, pencil, watercolor on paper
17¼ x 12¼ inches (438 x 311 mm)
Courtesy Michael Werner Gallery, New York and Cologne

Ism (Ismus), 2006
Feather pen, watercolor, India ink on paper
26⅛ x 20 inches (664 x 508 mm)
The Morgan Library & Museum; gift of the Modern and Contemporary Collectors' Committee; 2007.75

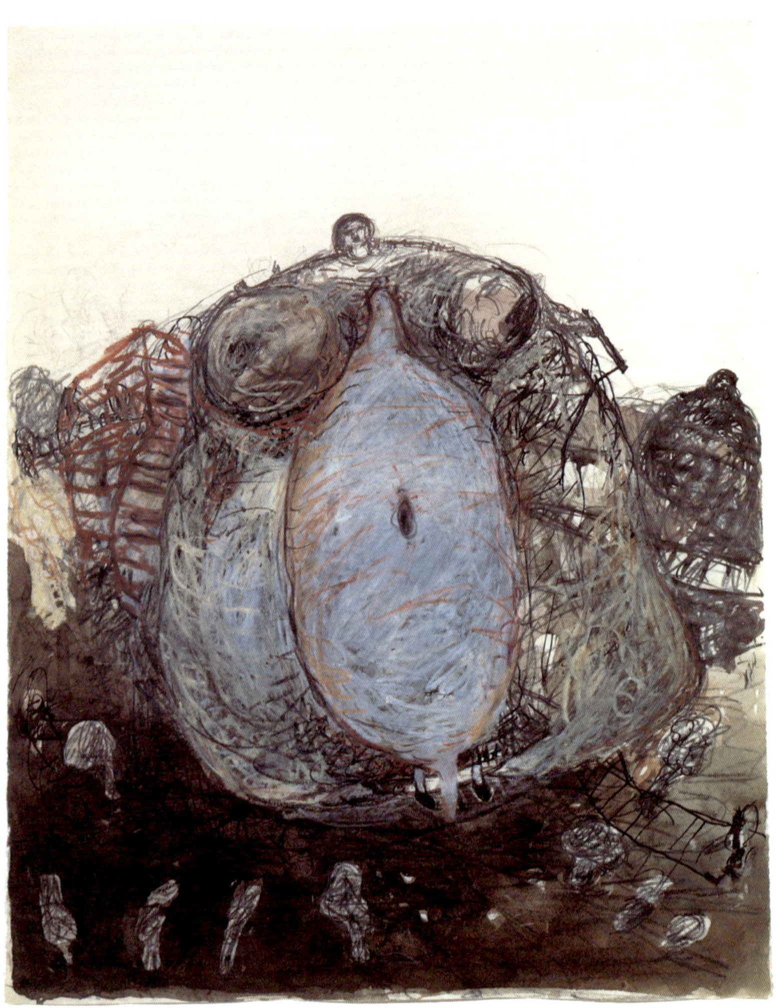

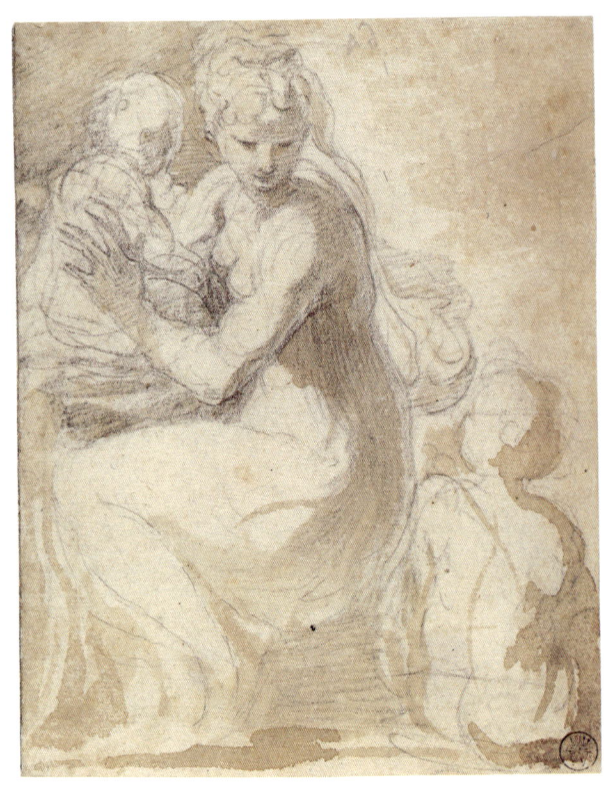

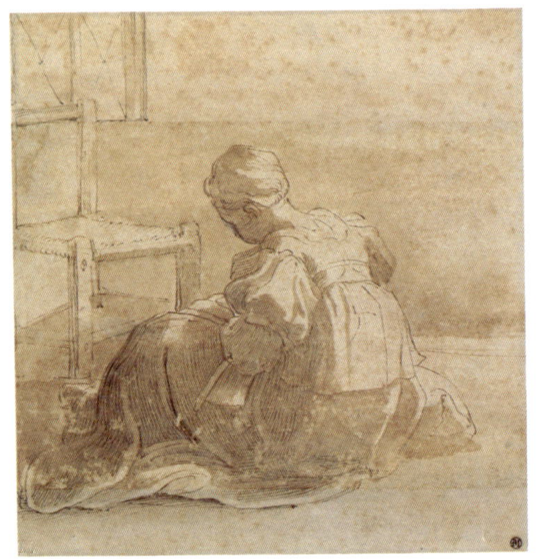

Clockwise from left:

Georg Baselitz, *The Whip Woman*, 1964

Parmigianino, *Virgin and Child with the Infant St. John the Baptist*, ca. 1527–31

Parmigianino, *Girl Seated on the Ground Near a Chair*, ca. 1524

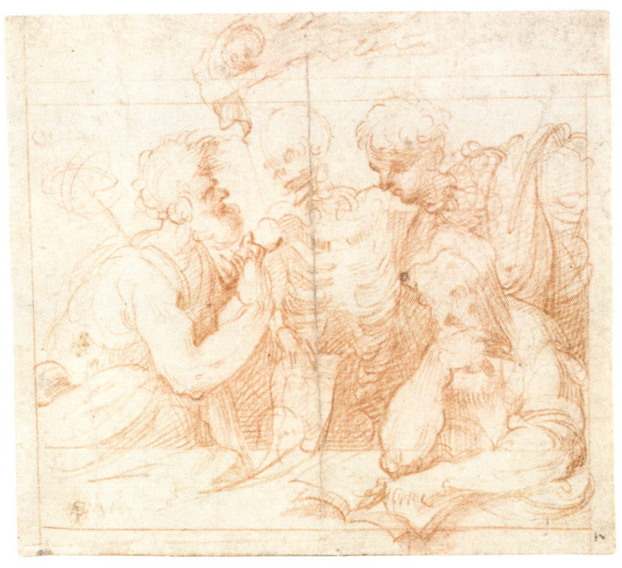

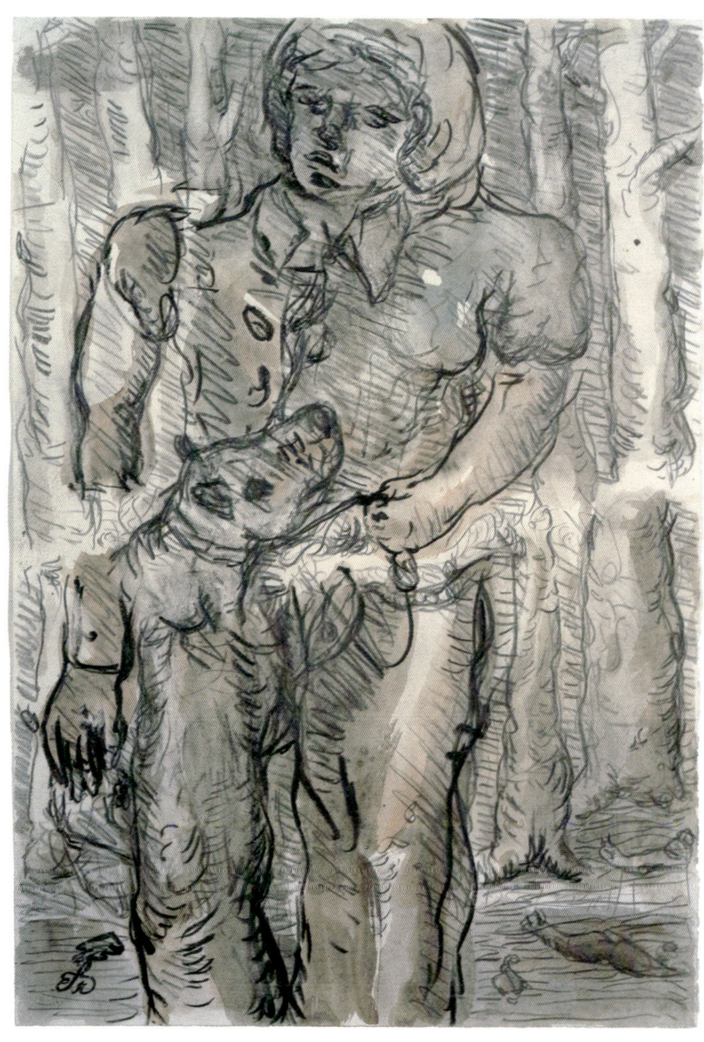

Attributed to Parmigianino, *Death Appearing to Three Philosophers,* ca. 1520–24

Georg Baselitz, *Kullervo, or Dog Boy,* 1966/67

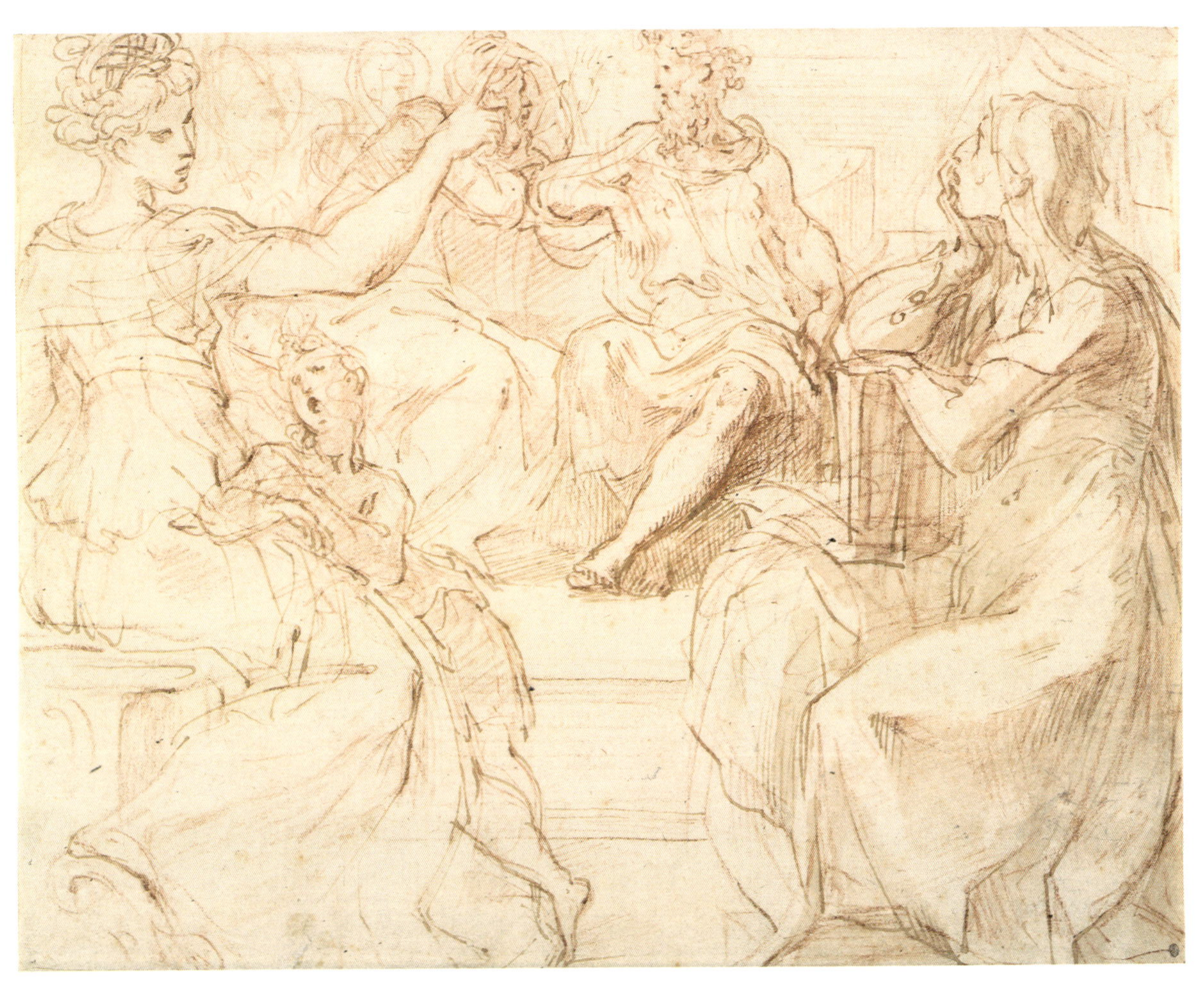

Parmigianino, *Study of Figures in the Foreground of the Marriage of the Virgin,* ca. 1526

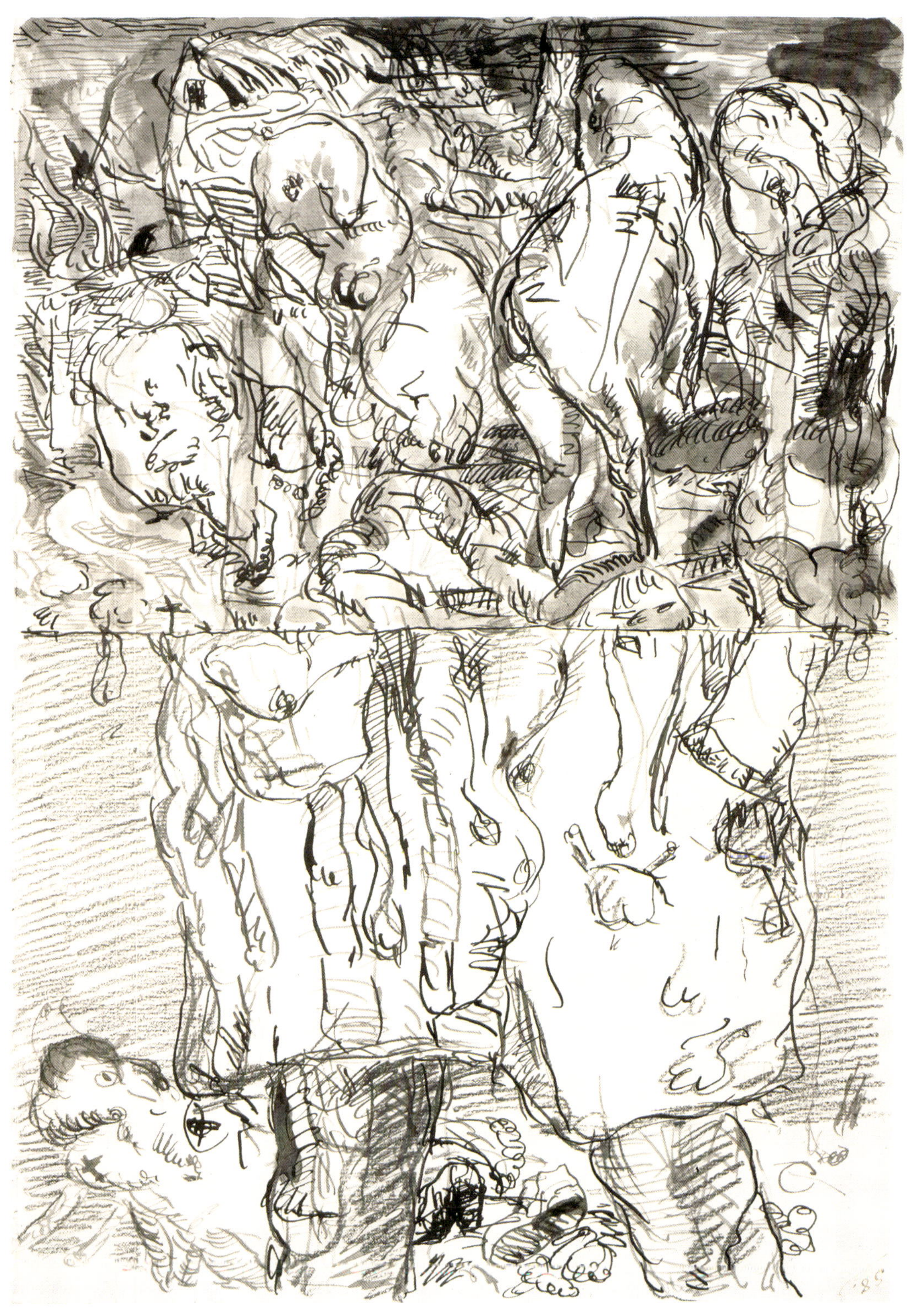

Georg Baselitz, *Untitled*, 1966/67

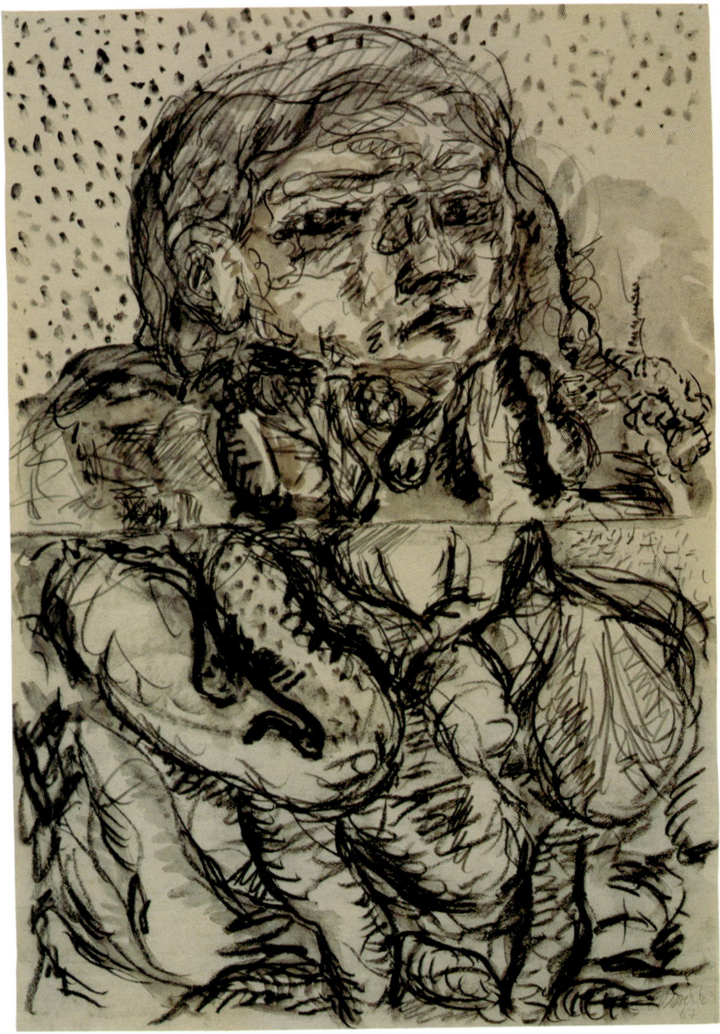

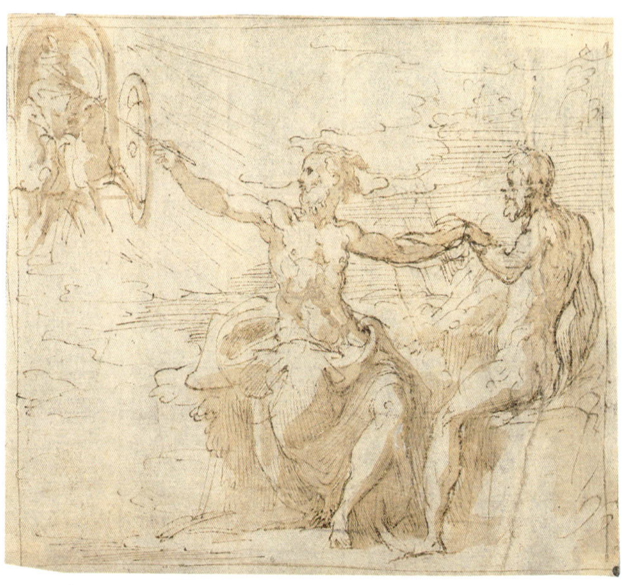

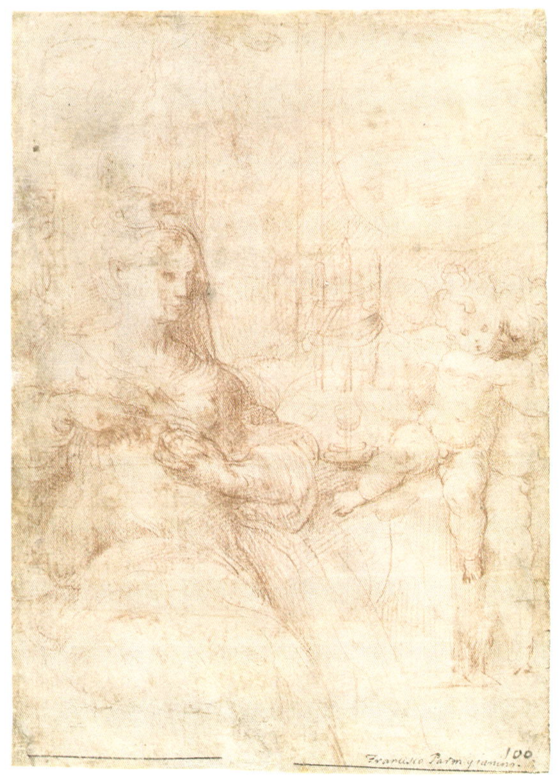

Clockwise from left:

Georg Baselitz, *Divided Hero,* 1966/67

Parmigianino, *Prometheus Animating Man,* ca. 1524–27

Parmigianino, *The Virgin Seated with Yarn Winder, and the Infant Christ Embracing the
Infant St. John,* early 1520s

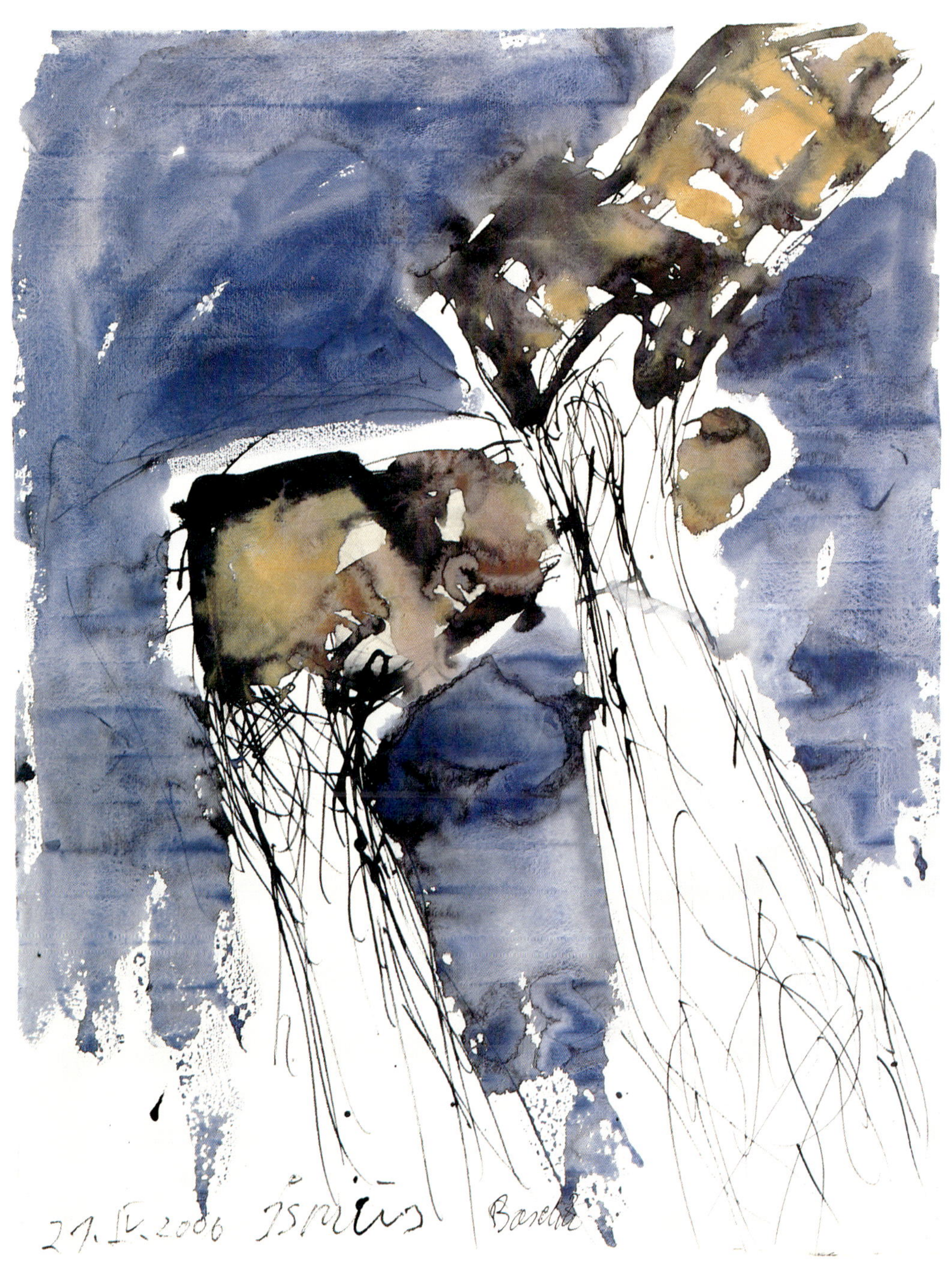

Georg Baselitz, *Ism,* 2006

Ellsworth Kelly

The drawings I've selected from the Morgan Library's collection include studies and sketches that concentrate on the action of the hand drawing with a pencil or ink stroke rather than a more finished drawing. I enjoy sketches that reveal how the artist sees and creates with a minimal amount of marks, whether it is a Rubens or a Matisse.

With my own drawings, whether figure or abstract or plant drawings, I prefer to draw quickly with line defining form with minimal shading. My abstract drawings are studies for further work as paintings and sculpture and are inspired by visual perceptions or distillations of forms in the world. My figure and plant drawings are drawn directly from a definite subject.

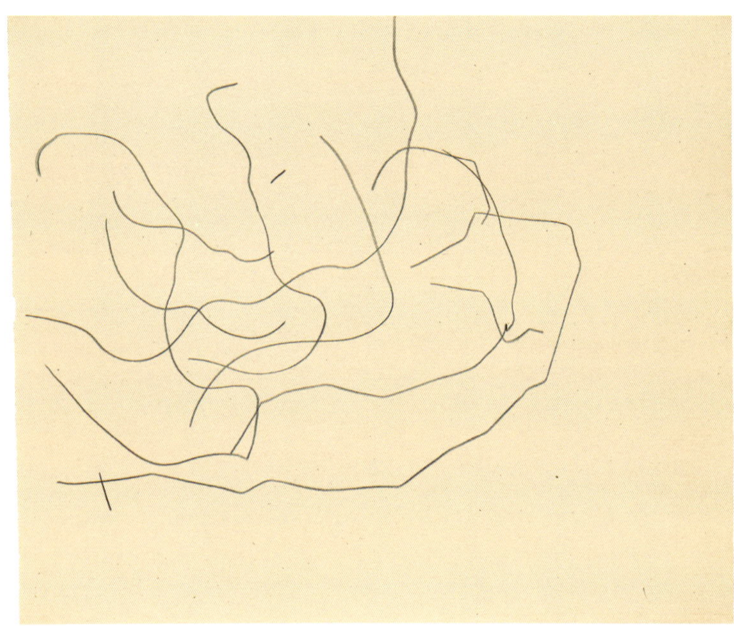

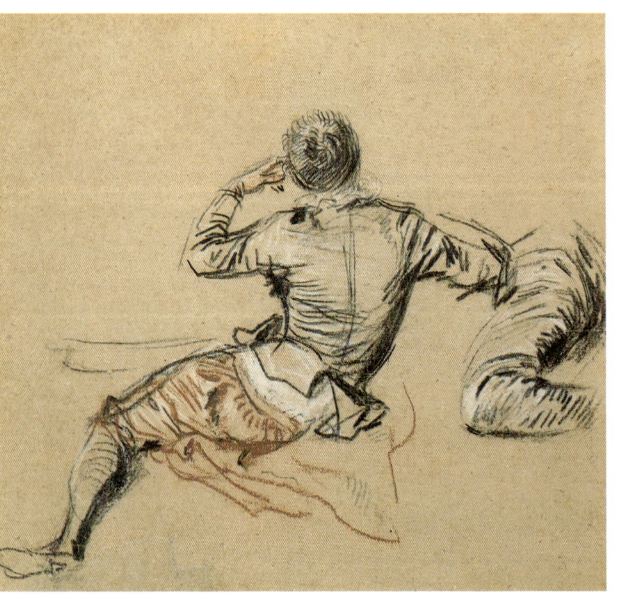

Ellsworth Kelly, *Pine Branches II,* 1950

Jean-Antoine Watteau, *Study of a Young Man Seen from the Back,* ca. 1717

Ellsworth Kelly was born in 1923 in Newburgh, New York. In the early 1940s, he studied at the Pratt Institute in Brooklyn. Inducted into the U.S. army in 1943, he was assigned to a camouflage unit and traveled to Europe. After the war, he attended the School of the Museum of Fine Arts in Boston for one year before moving to Paris. His formative years in France, from 1948 to 1954, were marked by numerous visits to museums and monuments, where he developed an interest in Romanesque and Byzantine art. From the start drawing was an important medium for Kelly, who explored on paper several concepts that would become essential to his art, such as chance (as in the surrealist technique of automatism) and the use of a grid. A keen observer of the world around him, he elaborated a distinctive form of abstraction based on details that caught his attention, for example, stripes on a beach cabana, patterns reflected on water, or the play of light and shadow on a building. He recorded such "fragments of vision," as he called them, in sketches and drawings that became the basis for paintings in which he distilled each form to its essence until its source was no longer recognizable. In the summer of 1949, Kelly created a series of drawings of plants, which he later saw as seminal to his formation: "The drawings from plant life seem to be a bridge to the way of seeing that brought about the paintings in 1949 that are the basis for all my later work."

Returning to the United States during the mid-1950s, Kelly lived in Manhattan among a community of artists that included Robert Indiana, Agnes Martin, and James Rosenquist. In 1956 he had his first New York solo exhibition at Betty Parsons Gallery. He continued his exploration of abstract art, first in multipanel works composed according to rules of combination and permutation, then in large paintings of elemental shapes in black and white or unmodulated colors. While his paintings and sculpture remained uncompromisingly abstract, Kelly's graphic production encompassed a wider range of modes of expression—from abstract collages to naturalist self-portraits. His major output on paper, however, consists of plant drawings, which he has continued to produce to this day, and in which, eschewing all emotion, he translates his perception of the world into pure form.

Selection of Old Master Drawings

Attributed to Peter Paul Rubens
(Flemish, 1577–1640)
Study of a Sleeping Lion, ca. 1614–15
Black chalk, heightened with white, on light gray paper
9¾ x 16½ inches (250 x 420 mm)
Purchased as the gift of the Fellows, with the special assistance of a number of Fellows and Trustees in honor of Miss Felice Stampfle; 1977.41

Attributed to Lucas Achtschellinck
(Flemish, 1626–1699)
A Copse of Birches in Winter, late seventeenth century
Black chalk, heightened with white, on light brown paper
11¹³⁄₁₆ x 7¹⁵⁄₁₆ inches (301 x 201 mm)
Purchased as the gift of Mrs. Carl Stern; 1988.32

Jean-Antoine Watteau
(French, 1684–1721)
Study of a Young Man Seen from the Back and Another Study of His Right Arm, ca. 1717
Black, red, white chalk on light brown paper
8³⁄₁₆ x 9 inches (208 x 227 mm)
Gift of Mr. and Mrs. Eugene V. Thaw; 2000.56

Jean-Auguste-Dominique Ingres
(French, 1780–1867)
Studies of Legs, Hands, and the Profile of a Head for the Martyrdom of St. Symphorien, ca. 1827–34
Black chalk and graphite on paper
18 x 12 inches (458 x 305 mm)
Purchased as the gift of Mrs. Charles Wrightsman; 1985.99

Edgar Degas
(French, 1834–1917)
Standing Man in a Bowler Hat, ca. 1870
Essence on brown oiled paper
12¾ x 7⅞ inches (323 x 201 mm)
Bequest of John S. Thacher; 1985.39

Vincent van Gogh
(Dutch, 1853–1890)
Wheat Field, Saint-Rémy de Provence, 1889
Steel and reed pens and brown ink on paper
18⅜ x 24⅜ inches (467 x 617 mm)
Gift of Mrs. Gerard B. Lambert in memory of Gerard B. Lambert; 1973.13

Henri Matisse
(French, 1869–1954)
Self-Portrait, 1945
Conté crayon on wove paper
16⁷⁄₁₆ x 12½ inches (418 x 317 mm)
Thaw Collection

Drawings by Ellsworth Kelly

Seaweed, 1949
Pencil on paper
22 x 17 inches (559 x 432 mm)
Private collection

Pine Branches II, 1950
Pencil on paper
16½ x 20¼ inches (419 x 514 mm)
Private collection

Untitled, 1962
Pencil on paper
28½ x 22½ inches (724 x 572 mm)
Private collection

Study for "Curve I," 1973
Pencil on paper
29 x 23 inches (737 x 584 mm)
Private collection

Allan Kelly, Sr. (After Death), 1982
Pencil on paper
11 x 13¾ inches (279 x 349 mm)
Private collection

Banana Leaf, 1992
Pencil on paper
20 x 30¼ inches (508 x 768 mm)
Private collection

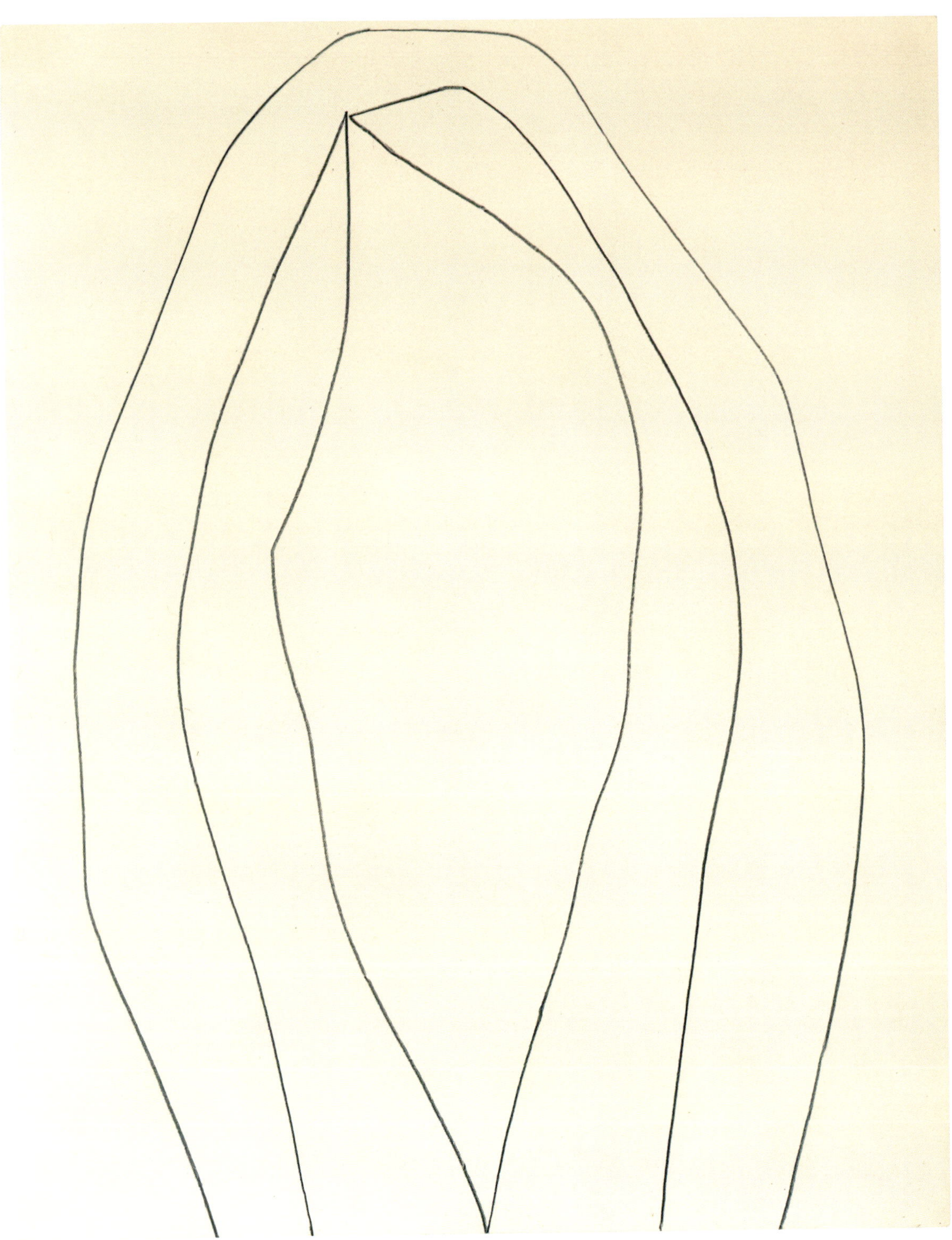

Ellsworth Kelly, *Untitled,* 1962

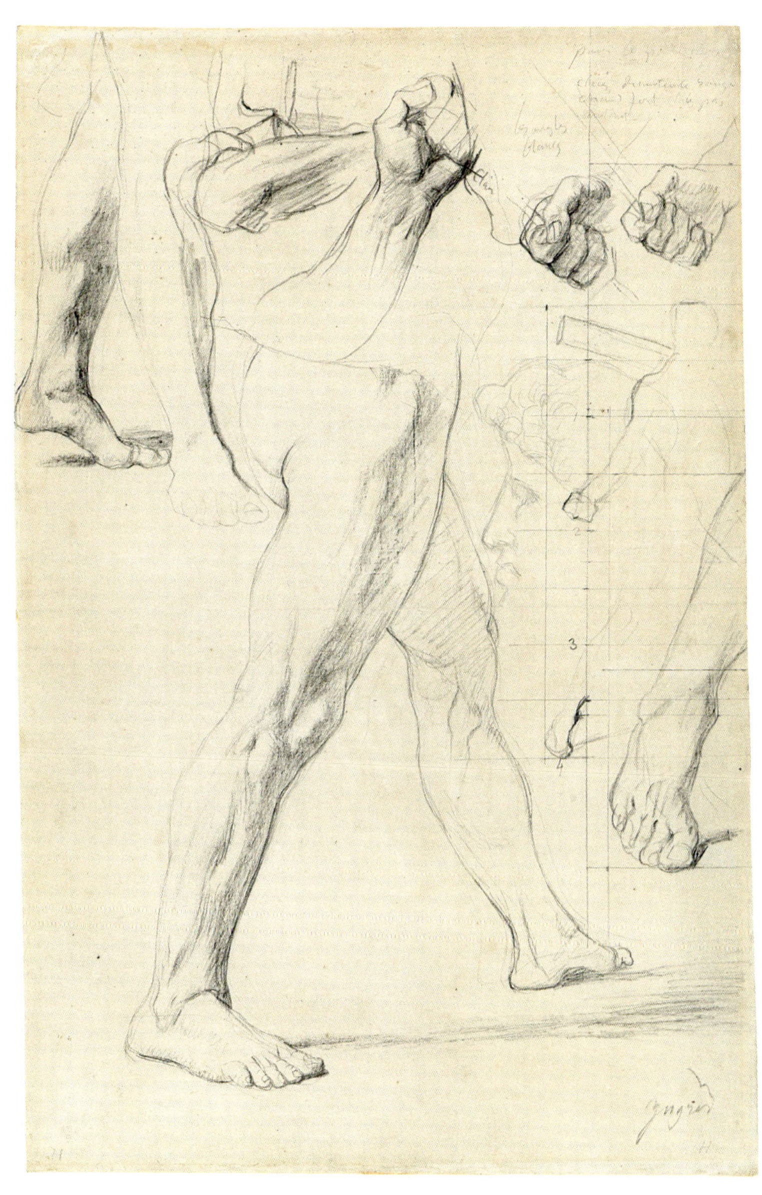

Jean-Auguste-Dominique Ingres, *Studies of Legs, Hands, and the Profile of a Head for the Martyrdom of St. Symphorien*, ca. 1827–34

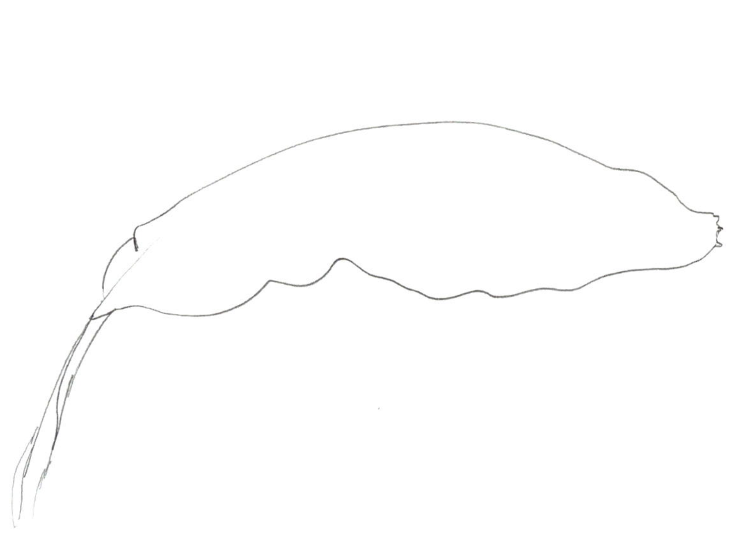

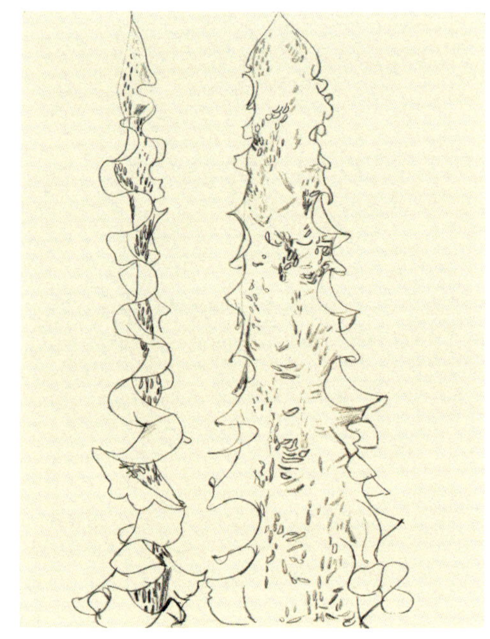

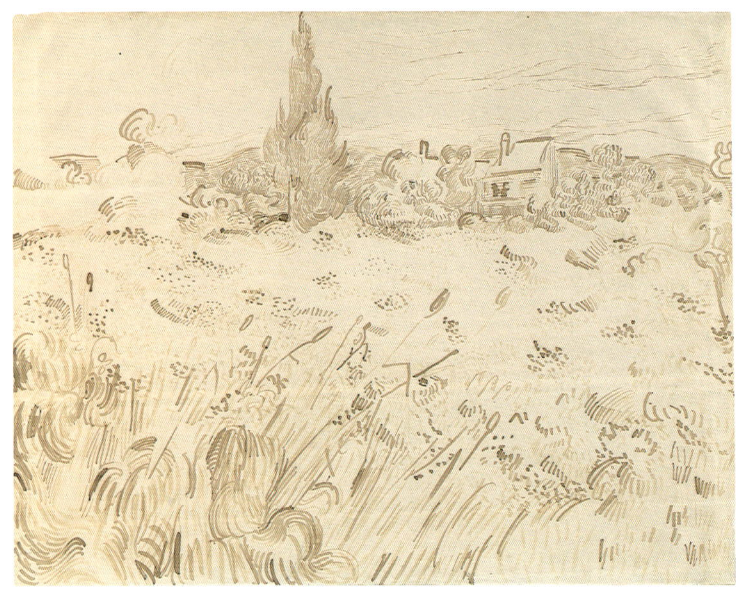

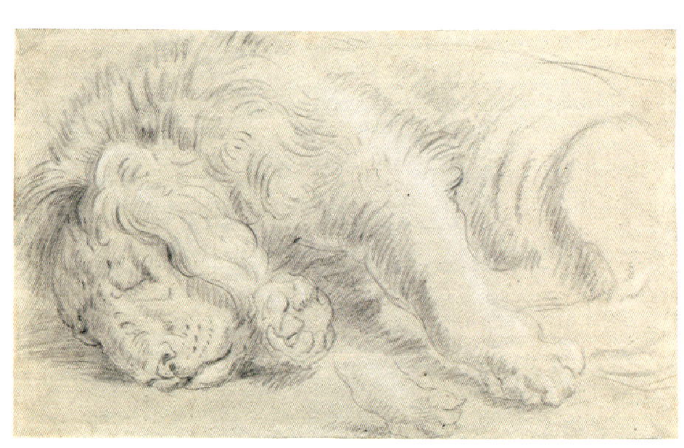

Clockwise from upper left:

Ellsworth Kelly, *Banana Leaf,* 1992

Ellsworth Kelly, *Seaweed,* 1949

Attributed to Peter Paul Rubens, *Study of a Sleeping Lion,* ca. 1614–15

Vincent van Gogh, *Wheat Field, Saint-Rémy de Provence,* 1889

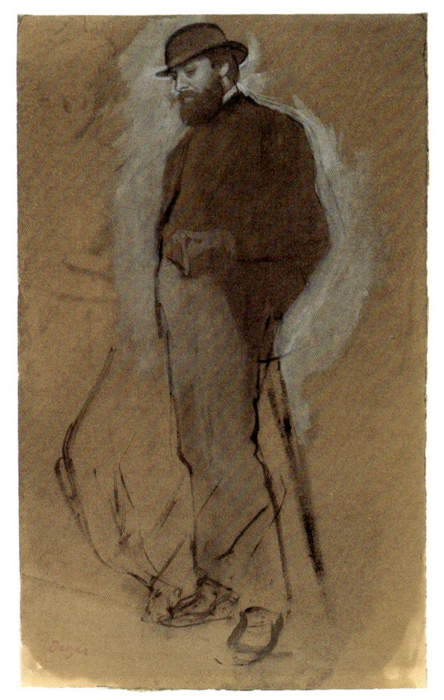

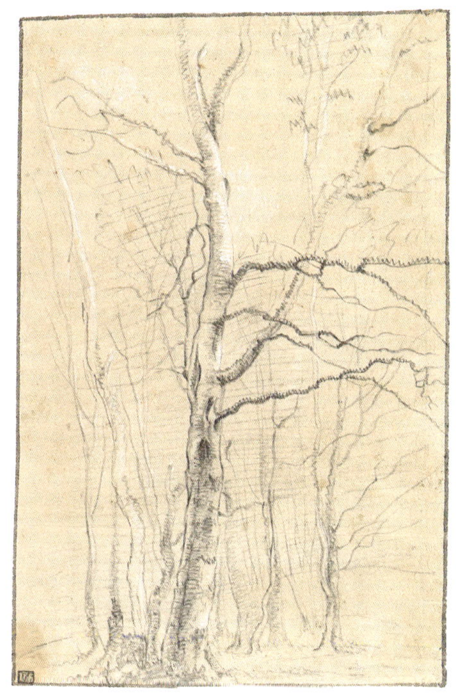

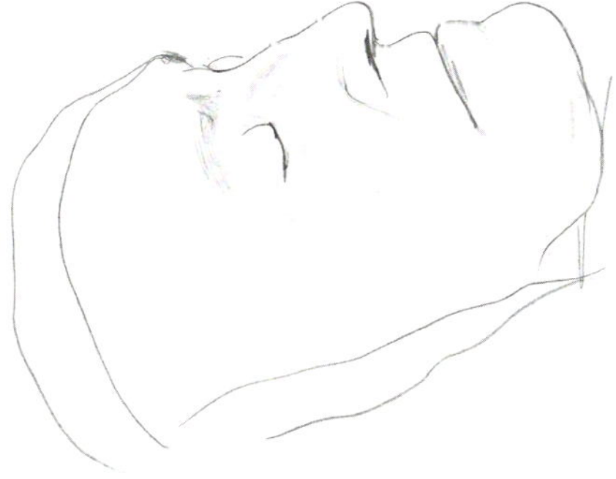

Clockwise from top:

Edgar Degas, *Standing Man in a Bowler Hat,* ca. 1870

Attributed to Lucas Achtschellinck, *A Copse of Birches in Winter,* late seventeenth century

Ellsworth Kelly, *Allan Kelly, Sr. (After Death),* 1982

Ellsworth Kelly, *Study for "Curve I,"* 1973

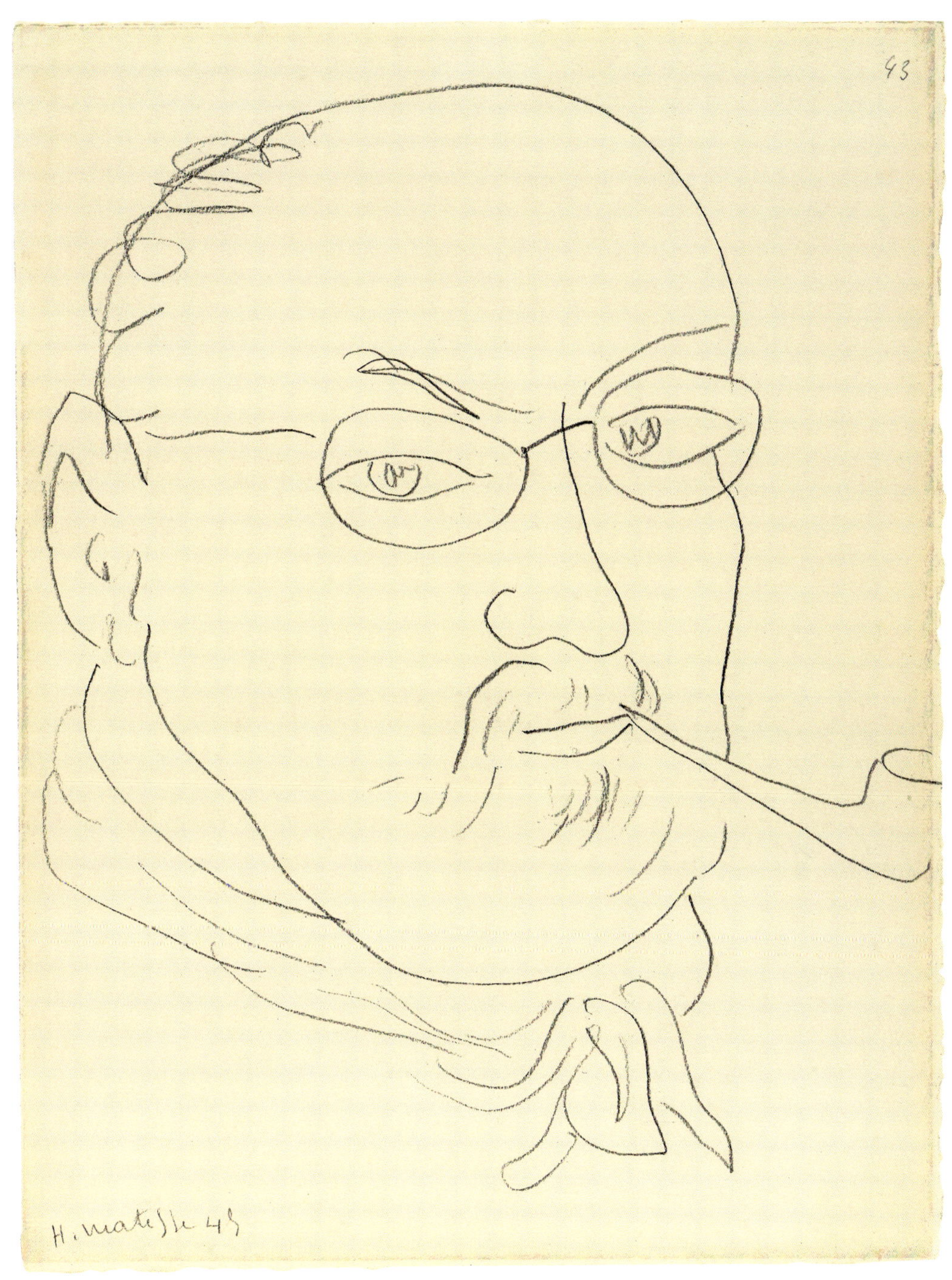

Henri Matisse, *Self-Portrait*, 1945

Giuseppe Penone

Drawings that are not concerned with style, or graphic character, or the artist's hand, but in which the act of drawing is the subject of the work, the means indispensable to the idea, the language, and the invention of the image. A drawing that is not so much about technical effect as it suggests a reflection on the world and offers an unexpected vision of reality.

1. Brueghel, Ribera, Piranesi, and my drawings on the growth of trees (pp. 32–33)

Nature dominates man, absorbs him, envelops him, makes him equal to all the elements that compose her. Man becomes nature as if he were her own creation and the individual dissolves himself into her.

2. Dürer, Mantegna, Perugino, and *The Imprint of Drawing* (pp. 34–35)

The attempt to control and investigate the material, to rationalize and understand nature through a work whose technique makes her objective, describes and rationalizes the mystery and the spirituality that emanate from her.

3. Bernini, Cézanne, Klimt, and *Skin of Graphite* (pp. 36–37)

Abandoning himself to the material of the drawing, to provoke it and to suggest it through the mark that underlines and reveals the weave of the paper, or with the light stain of watercolor absorbed by the paper, or with the line that, repeated, surrounds and reveals the subject hypnotizing the gaze . . . the artist reveals the sensuality of nature.

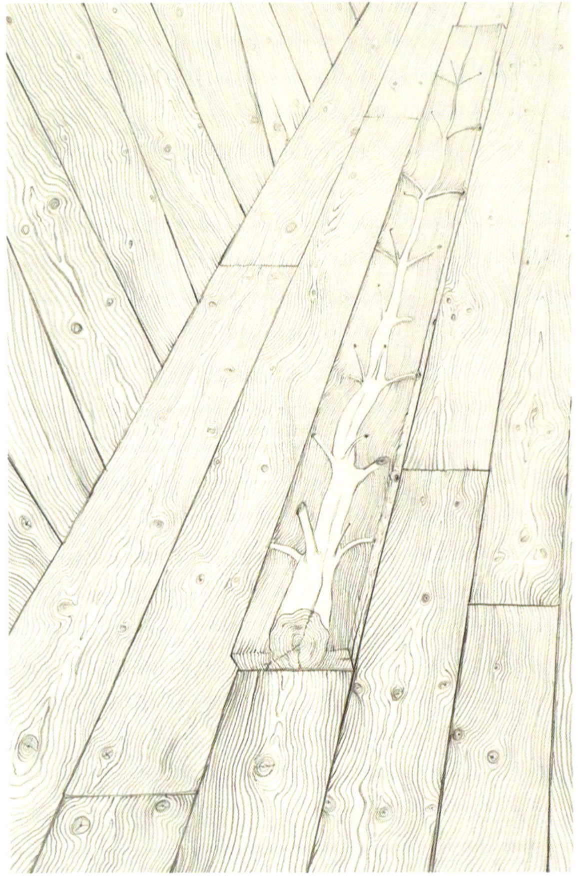

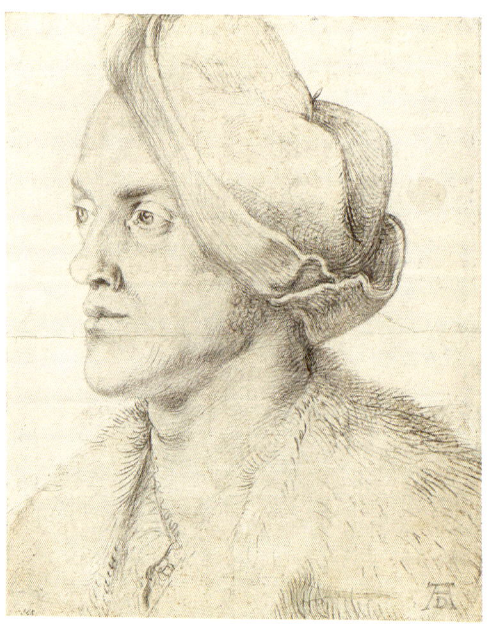

Giuseppe Penone, *Study for "15-Year-Old Tree,"* 1970

Albrecht Dürer, *Portrait of the Artist's Brother Endres,* ca. 1518

Giuseppe Penone was born in 1947 in the village of Garessio, south of Turin, and lived on the family farm until 1966, when he moved to Turin to study sculpture at the Accademia di Belle Arte. In the late 1960s, he was associated with the Arte Povera (Poor Art) movement, a loosely knit group of Italian artists who rejected artistic conventions in their sculpture, installations, and performances by using nonartistic, everyday gestures and materials. (Other members included Alighiero Boetti, Jannis Kounellis, and Mario Merz.) From the beginning, Penone's work has dealt primarily with nature, time, and the relationship of man to nature through trans-fusion of energy and metamorphosis of human and vegetal forms. Many of his pieces were real-ized outdoors and result from his direct inter-vention on natural processes, as when he locally altered the growth of a tree by placing an iron cast of his hand on the trunk.

Sculpture and drawing have been Penone's primary mediums and are closely related through their processes. Both often involve the artist making a mark or an impression with his own body on some type of support, such as clay or paper, a heap of leaves on the ground, or a strip of adhesive tape from which the impression can be projected onto the wall. Penone developed the concept of drawing as the record of a trace. "Drawing is the organization in space of a dirty material," he said. A large number of his draw-ings are based on the imprint of his skin, either by direct contact, for instance in drawings based on his fingerprints, or indirectly, as in the enlargement of the imprint of his eyelid on a forty-eight-foot-wide drawing made of almond-shaped sheets of unwoven fiber, which suggest a pattern of leaves. In a major series of ten draw-ings, executed in 2002–3, using each of his fin-gerprints as a starting point, Penone extended each line of the fingerprint until the entire design resembled the growth rings of an ancient tree, in a beautiful visualization of the fusion of man and tree that has always been at the core of his art.

Selection of Old Master Drawings

Attributed to Pieter Bruegel
(Netherlandish, ca. 1525–1569)
Mountain Landscape with a River, Village, and Castle, ca. 1555
Pen and two colors of brown ink, brown wash on paper; framing line in brown ink
14⅛ x 17⅝ inches (357 x 446 mm)
Purchased with the assistance of the Fellows; 1952.25

José de Ribera
(Spanish, 1588?–1652)
Marsyas Bound to a Tree, ca. 1630s
Red chalk on paper
9 ¹⁵⁄₁₆ x 7 ⁹⁄₁₆ inches (252 x 192 mm)
Purchased as the gift of Mr. Frederick R. Koch; 1976.48

Giovanni Battista Piranesi
(Italian, 1720–1778)
Prison Interior of a Great Hall with Piers and Arches Pierced by Grated Oculi, and Figures in Foreground, ca. 1740–50
Pen and brown ink, with gray and brown wash, over black chalk on paper; framing line in pen and brown ink
7⅕ x 9 ⁱ¹⁄₁₆ inches (183 x 246 mm)
Bequest of Junius S. Morgan and gift of Henry S. Morgan; 1966.11:16

After Perugino
(Italian, ca. 1450–1523)
Study for the Head of St. Lawrence, ca. 1496–1520
Metalpoint, brush and red ink, brown wash, heightened with white gouache, on light brown prepared paper
8⅞ x 6⅞ inches (224 x 173 mm)
Gift of J. P. Morgan, Jr., 1924; I, 10

After Andrea Mantegna
(Italian, 1431–1506)
Bacchanal with a Wine Vat, ca. 1500
Pen and brown ink on paper
11 x 16⅜ inches (282 x 416 mm)
Gift of Mr. Janos Scholz; 1981.86

Albrecht Dürer
(German, 1471–1528)
Portrait of the Artist's Brother Endres, ca. 1518
Charcoal on paper; background later washed with white lead
12¾ x 10¼ inches (324 x 262 mm)
Gift of Mrs. Alexander Perry Morgan in memory of Alexander Perry Morgan; 1973.17

Gian Lorenzo Bernini
(Italian, 1598–1680)
Portrait of Cardinal Borghese, ca. 1632
Red chalk, over graphite, on paper
9 ¹⁵⁄₁₆ x 7¼ inches (253 x 184 mm)
Gift of J. P. Morgan, Jr., 1924; IV, 176

Paul Cézanne
(French, 1839–1906)
Bare Trees by a River, ca. 1900–1904
Watercolor on paper
12⅜ x 19¼ inches (312 x 487 mm)
Thaw Collection

Gustav Klimt
(Austrian, 1862–1918)
Seated Woman with Raised Skirt, ca. 1909–10
Graphite pencil on wove paper
22⅛ x 14⅝ inches (561 x 371 mm)
Bequest of Fred Ebb; 2005.142

Drawings by Giuseppe Penone

Study for "To Adhere to the Trees" (Progetto per "aderire agli alberi"), 1968
Ink on paper
11 ¹¹⁄₁₆ x 15¾ inches (300 x 400 mm)
Collection of the artist

I Feel the Respiration of the Forest . . . Study for "Maritime Alps—It Will Continue to Grow Except at that Point" (Sento il respiro della foresta . . . Progetto per "Alpi Marittime—Continuerà a crescere tranne che in quel punto"), 1968
Ink and graphite on paper
19 ¹¹⁄₁₆ x 13¾ inches (500 x 350 mm)
Collection of the artist

The Tree Will Remember the Contact (L'albero conserva nella sua crescita la memoria del contatto), 1968
Ink on paper
11 ¹¹⁄₁₆ x 15¾ inches (300 x 400 mm)
Collection of the artist

Study for "15-Year-Old Tree" (Progetto per un "albero di 15 anni"), 1970
Graphite on paper
22¼ x 15 inches (565 x 381 mm)
Courtesy Marian Goodman Gallery, New York

The Imprint of Drawing, Right Ring Finger (L'impronta del disegno, Anulare destro), 2001
Graphite and etching ink on paper
84⅝ x 55⅛ inches (2,150 x 1,400 mm)
The Morgan Library & Museum; gift of the Modern and Contemporary Collectors' Committee; 2007.78

Skin of Graphite "Reflection of Jade 1" (Pelle di grafite "Riflesso di giadeite 1"), 2005
Graphite on black paper
39⅜ x 59 ¹⁄₁₆ inches (1,000 x 1,500 mm)
Collection of the artist

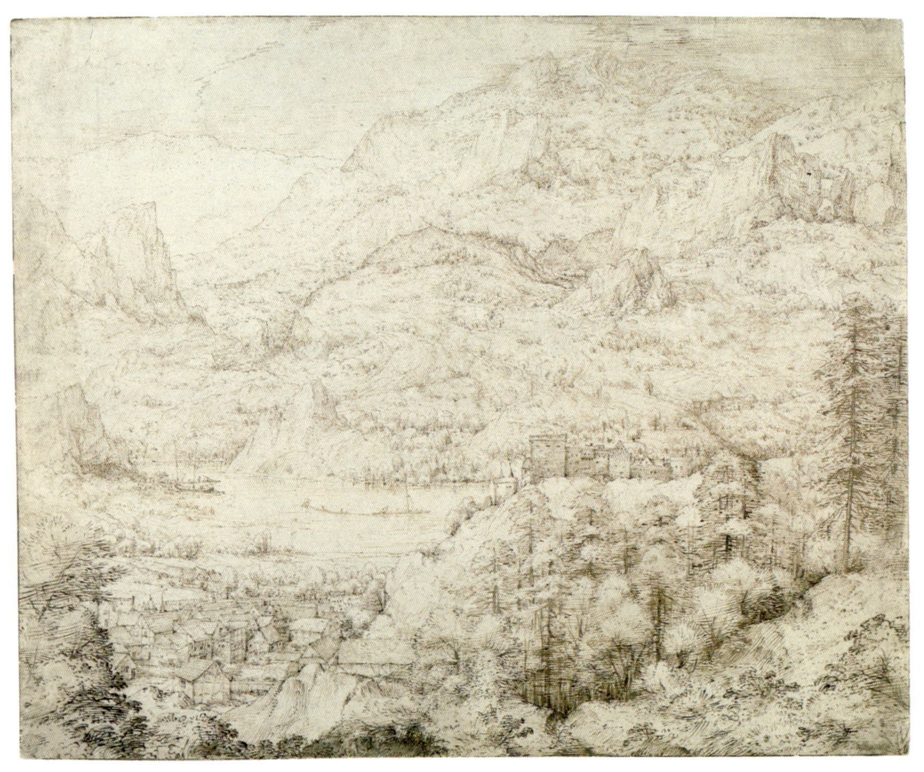

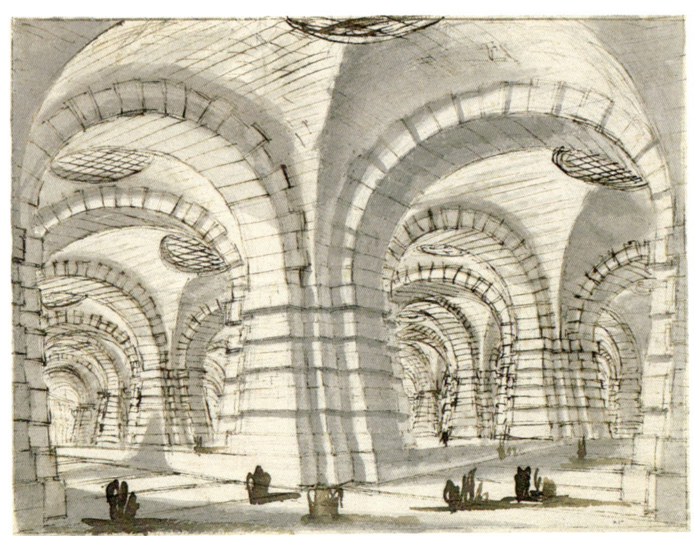

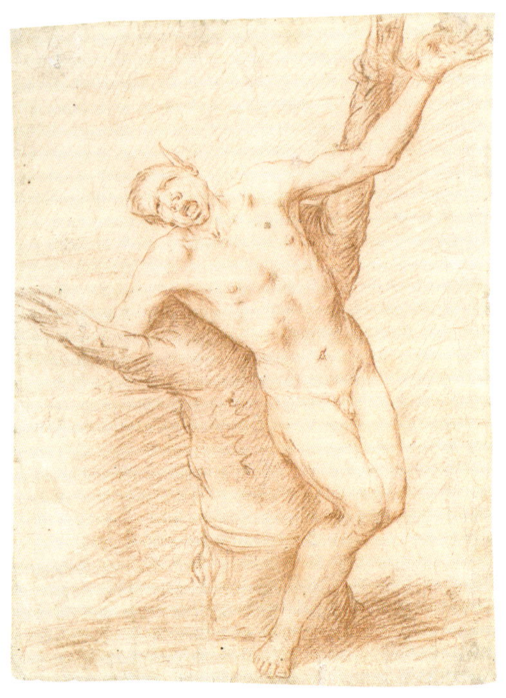

Clockwise from top:

Attributed to Pieter Bruegel, *Mountain Landscape with a River, Village, and Castle,* ca. 1555

José de Ribera, *Marsyas Bound to a Tree,* ca. 1630s

Giovanni Battista Piranesi, *Prison Interior of a Great Hall with Piers and Arches Pierced by Grated Oculi,* ca. 1740–50

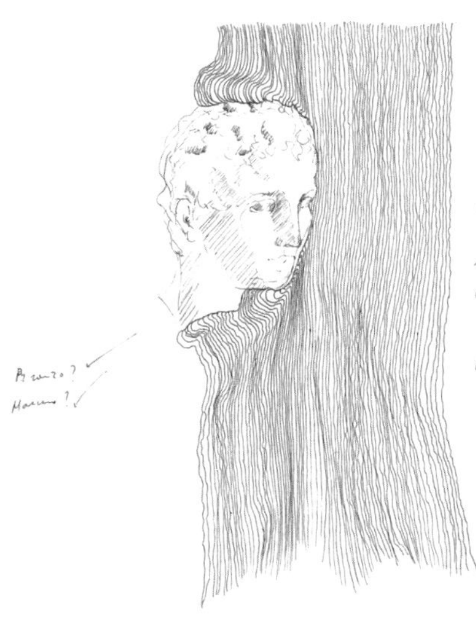

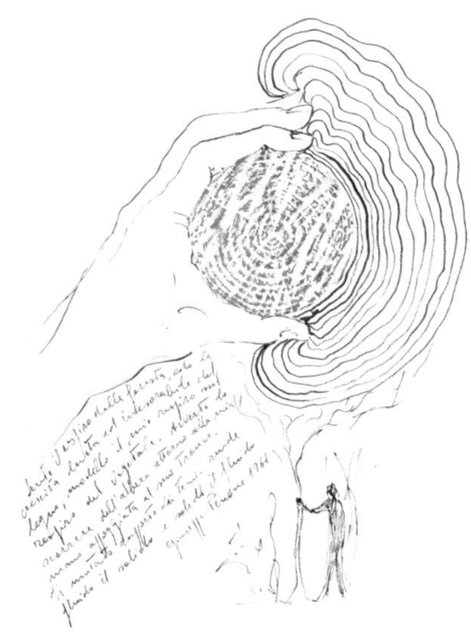

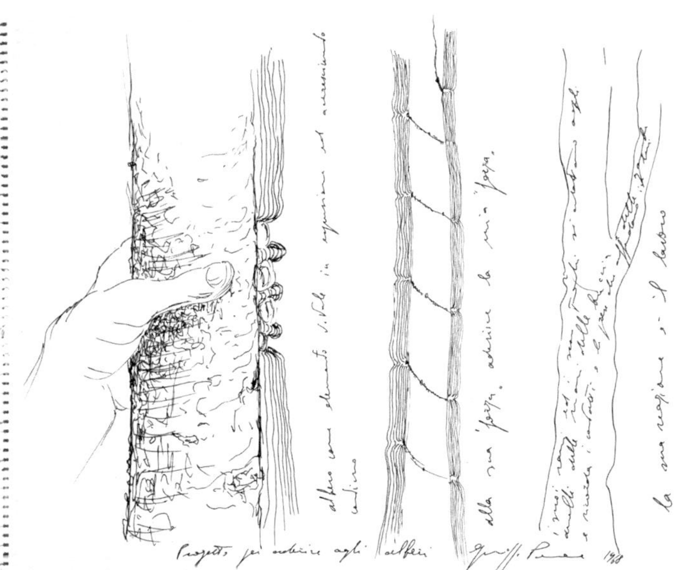

Clockwise from upper left:

Giuseppe Penone, *The Tree Will Remember the Contact,* 1968

Giuseppe Penone, *I Feel the Respiration of the Forest . . . ,* 1968

Giuseppe Penone, *Study for "To Adhere to the Trees,"* 1968

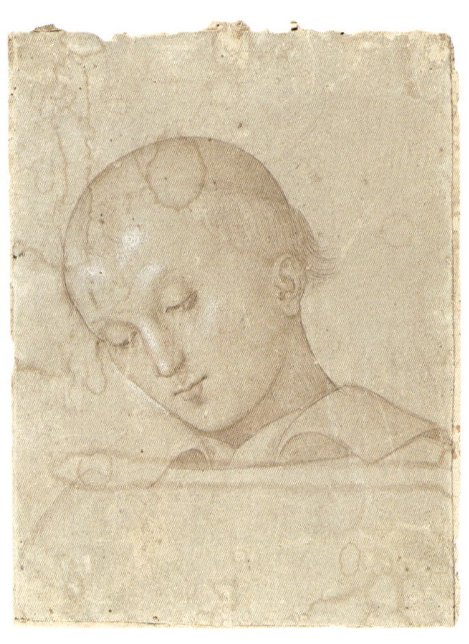

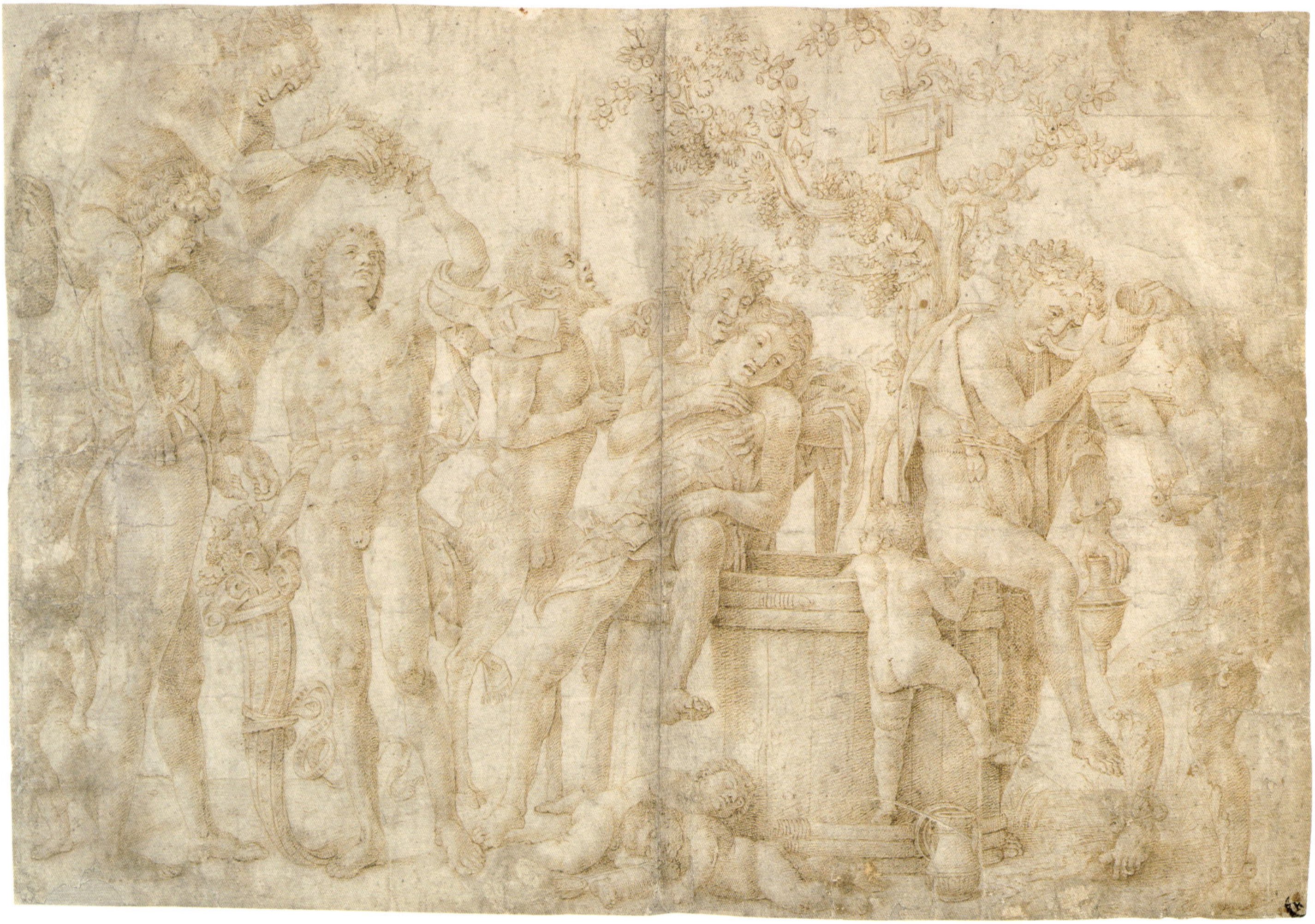

Above:

After Perugino, *Study for the Head of St. Lawrence,* ca. 1496–1520

After Andrea Mantegna, *Bacchanal with a Wine Vat,* ca. 1500

Opposite:

Giuseppe Penone, *The Imprint of Drawing, Right Ring Finger,* 2001

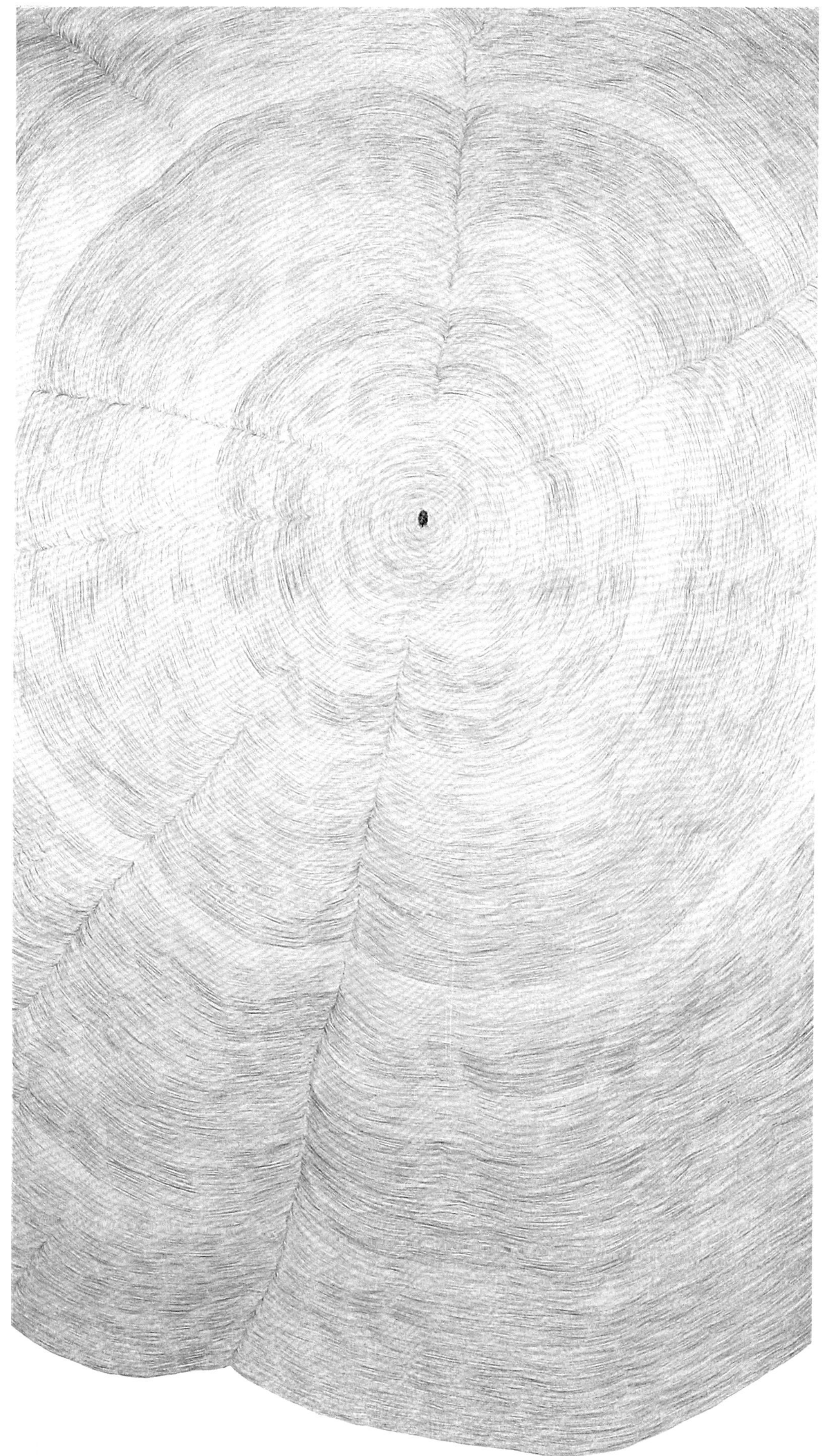

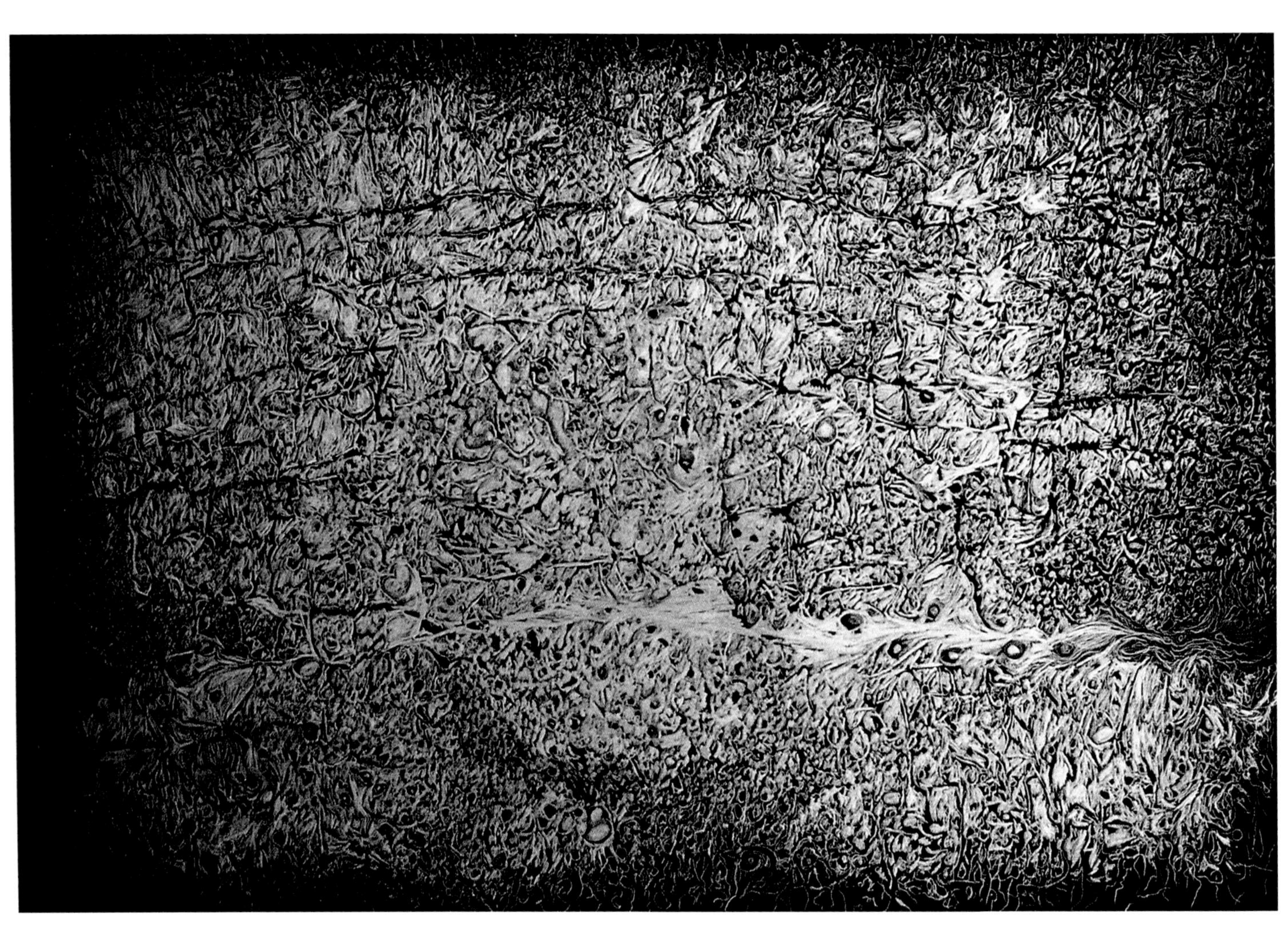

Giuseppe Penone, *Skin of Graphite "Reflection of Jade 1,"* 2005

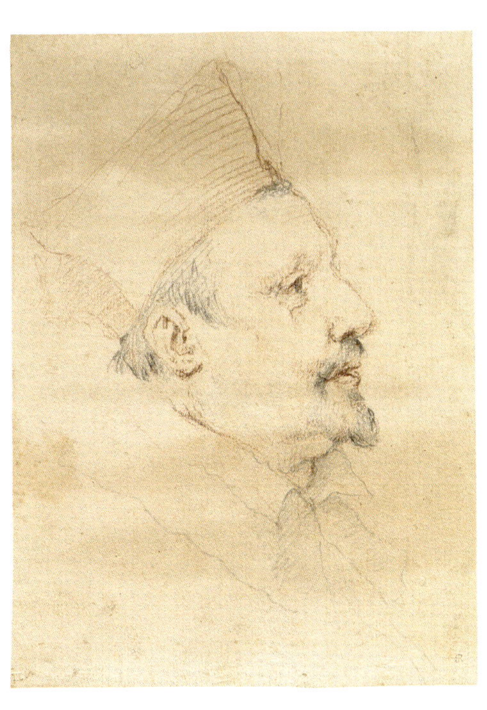

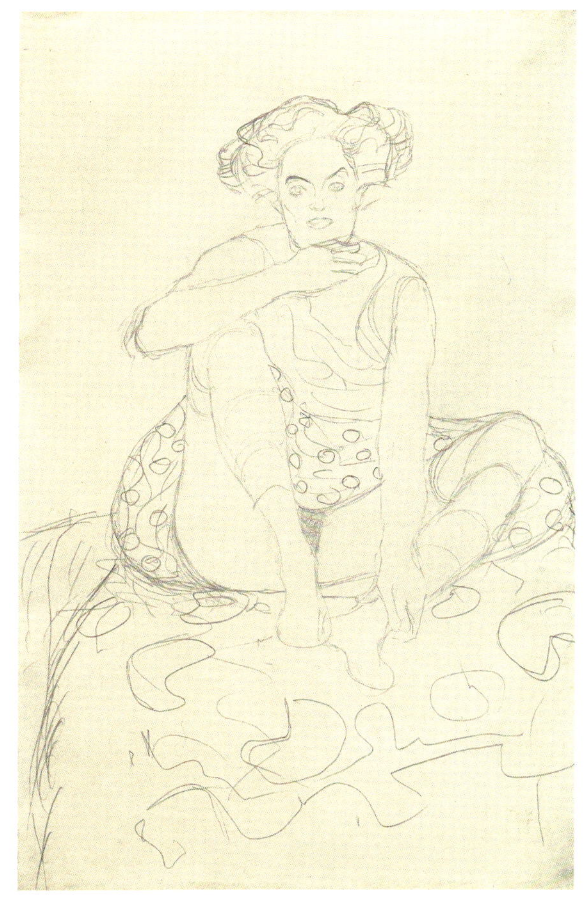

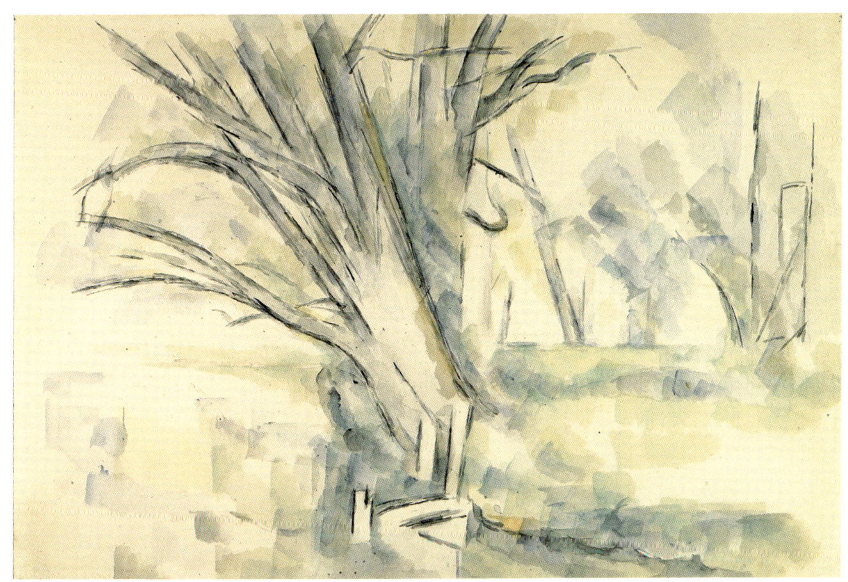

Clockwise from upper left:

Gian Lorenzo Bernini, *Portrait of Cardinal Borghese*, ca. 1632

Gustav Klimt, *Seated Woman with Raised Skirt*, ca. 1909–10

Paul Cézanne, *Bare Trees by a River*, ca. 1900–1904

Dorothea Rockburne

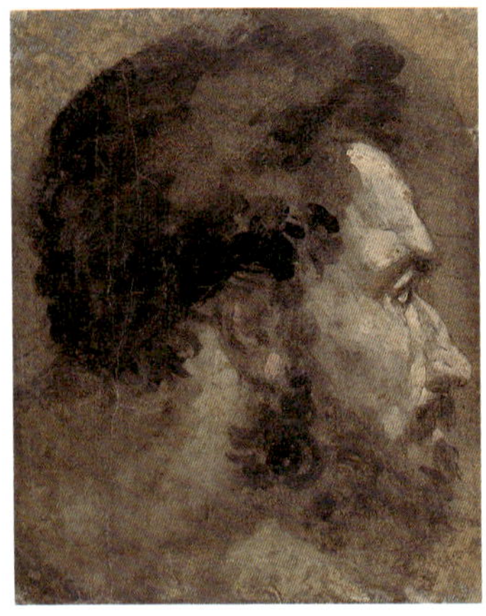

Drawing is as fundamental to my art making as my skeleton is to my body. Drawing is the bones of my thought, the crank that allows me to understand the invention of art. The art of ancient Egypt, the Renaissance, mannerism, Russian constructivism, and mathematics have all profoundly affected me.

My work diaries go back forty-one years. They chart the history of my thinking:

1966

Drawing is the engine that drives my painting.

1970

I've never separated the cerebral from the emotional. It's not a separate activity. I think best when I'm emotionally clear.

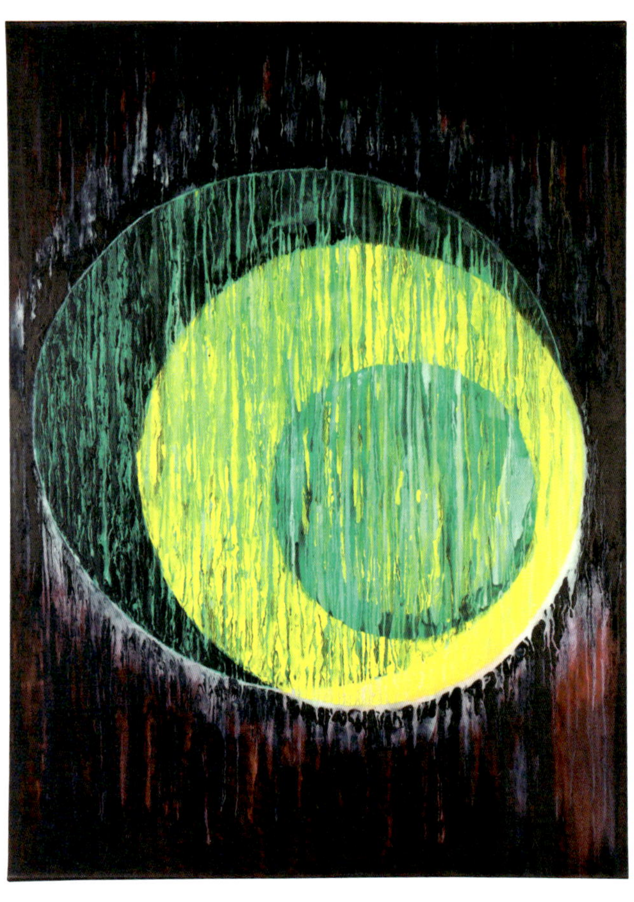

1973: Notes on Drawing Procedures

1. How could drawing be of itself and not about something else?

2. Construct an investigation of drawing based on information contained within the paper and not on any other information.

3. Thought acts upon itself.

4. It seems reasonable that paper acting upon itself through its own implied geometry could become a subject-object.

1978

When I make a work I want to be surprised by it. I want to be changed by having made it. If I'm not surprised I'll discard it. The creation process is magical. . . . In the *Conservation Drawings,* at the point where the rectangle is folded and the interior formation is found, I originally had no idea how it would be assembled until I did it. Yet, within the work logic, there's only one way it could have been reassembled.

1991

Cézanne studied Mont Sainte-Victoire; I study the cosmos. The challenge lies in translating information into the structure of art.

2004

Mannerist drawing and painting deeply moves and influences my work. Pushing formalism to the point of radicalism, the mannerists reacted against previous ideas of perspective and color. Instead of a vanishing point perspective, they chose to distort, elongate, and exaggerate form. Employing an accurate painting of emotions, they often reached beyond formal restrictions into a mystic dimension.

2007

Prime Partition Three, 2006, *The Conjecture,* 2007: curves in transition from one to four imagined dimensions.

Domenico Beccafumi, *Head of a Bearded Man in Profile to the Right,* 1530s

Dorothea Rockburne, *Prime Partition Three,* 2006

Dorothea Rockburne was born in Verdun, Quebec, in 1932 and received her first artistic training at the École des Beaux-Arts in Montreal. In the early 1950s, she studied at the experimental Black Mountain College in North Carolina, taking classes in mathematics and philosophy as well as art. The innovative teaching methods of Black Mountain and the relationships Rockburne formed there with professors and fellow students were crucial to her formation. In 1955 she moved to New York City, where she has lived ever since. From her experience as a dancer and her participation in performances, she developed her conception of art as a process. "I am doing the things to the material that when I danced I did with my body," she said in 1995. From her first installations, in the late 1960s, mathematics and physics have been a major source of inspiration. In an early series of multipart works based on set theory, she visualized organizing principles and abstract relationships by combining sheets of cardboard, paper, and crude oil. Disregarding the traditional distinctions between drawing, painting, and sculpture, she spread these pieces over the wall and onto the floor. Subsequent series dealt with different mathematical concepts, such as the golden section, non-Euclidean geometry, and Mandelbrot's equation.

Rockburne's primary medium is paper of all kinds, from carbon paper and Kraft paper to vellum and papyrus. In creating a piece, she is guided by the properties of the material. This approach led to the groundbreaking series of the early 1970s, Drawing Which Makes Itself, in which each drawing was self-generated by folding the paper according to a geometric rule.

Several sojourns in Italy, notably at the American Academy in Rome in 1991, have fueled Rockburne's interest in Italian art, especially from the early Renaissance (Giotto, Piero della Francesca) and the sixteenth century (Pontormo, Tintoretto). A mural of the skies, with planets and constellations, in a seventeenth-century Italian villa spurred her interest in astronomy, which has remained central to her work since the early 1990s and found a major expression in the mural paintings on a cosmological theme that she created for the headquarters of Sony USA in New York in 1992. The chromatic richness and sensuousness of Rockburne's recent works based on astronomy underscore the subtle balance between intuition, emotion, and rigorous intellectual thought on which all of her work is predicated.

Selection of Old Master Drawings

Domenico Beccafumi
(Italian, 1486 – 1551)

Head of an Old Man with Open Mouth,
ca. 1529 – 35
Egg tempera on brown paper; outlines indented; varnished
11¼ x 8 inches (285 x 203 mm)
Gift of J. P. Morgan, Jr., 1924; I, 19b

Head of a Bearded Man in Profile to the Right,
1530s
Egg tempera on brown paper; outlines indented; varnished
10 x 8⅛ inches (254 x 206 mm)
Gift of J. P. Morgan, Jr., 1924; I, 19a

Tintoretto
(Italian, 1518 – 1594)

So-called *Head of Emperor Vitellius,* 1540 – 80
Charcoal, heightened with white chalk, on blue paper faded to brown
13¹⁄₁₆ x 9¹¹⁄₁₆ inches (333 x 249 mm)
Gift of Mr. and Mrs. Carl Stern; 1959.17

Man Climbing into a Boat, ca. 1579
Charcoal on paper; framing lines in brown ink
12⅜ x 8 inches (313 x 203 mm)
Gift of J. P. Morgan, Jr., 1924; IV, 76

Guido Reni
(Italian, 1575 – 1642)

Study of Forearms with Hands Crossed,
ca. 1613 – 14
Black and red chalk, heightened with white chalk, on paper
6⁵⁄₁₆ x 11¾ inches (160 x 299 mm)
Gift of Mr. Janos Scholz; 1980.7

Guercino
(Italian, 1591 – 1666)

Galatea Accompanied by Two Tritons,
ca. 1650 – 60
Red chalk on paper
14½ x 18 inches (368 x 457 mm)
Gift of J. P. Morgan, Jr., 1924; IV, 168i

Circle of Jacopo da Pontormo
(Italian, 1494 – ca. 1556)

Right Arm and Hand, with Palm Turned Upward
Red chalk on paper
3¼ x 5½ inches (78 x 141 mm)
Gift of J. P. Morgan, Jr., 1924; IV, 21a

Lower Right Arm with Sleeve, Casting a Shadow
Red chalk on paper
3¹⁄₁₆ x 6⅜ inches (78 x 162 mm)
Gift of J. P. Morgan, Jr., 1924; IV, 21b

Drawings by Dorothea Rockburne

Conservation Class #5, 1973
Strathmore 2 ply and graphite
49 x 42 inches (framed; 1,244 x 1,066 mm)
Collection of Christine Williams

Conservation Class #9, 1973
Strathmore 2 ply and graphite
34¼ x 70 inches (framed; 876 x 1,778 mm)
Collection of Christine Williams

Dark Angel: Elephant, 1982
Watercolor, pencil, vellum, glue on fiberglass and aluminum honeycomb panel
32¾ x 31 inches (framed; 832 x 787 mm)
Collection of the artist

The Plan of St. Gall, 1988 – 89
60 x 50¼ inches (1,524 x 1,276 mm)
Gold leaf, acetate, watercolor and ragboard, waterleaf paper, stitchery tape
Private collection

Prime Partition Three, 2006
Watercolor on Dura-Lar
40 x 30 inches (1,016 x 762 mm)
Courtesy Greenberg Van Doren Gallery, New York

The Conjecture, 2007
Watercolor on Dura-Lar
50 x 35 inches (1,270 x 889 mm)
Courtesy Greenberg Van Doren Gallery, New York

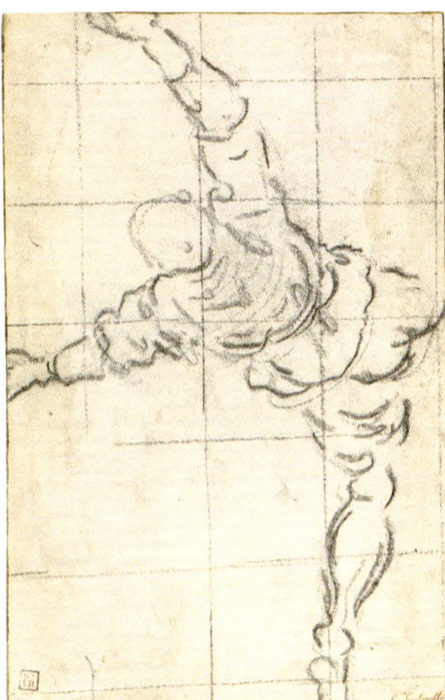

Dorothea Rockburne, *Conservation Class #5,* 1973

Tintoretto, *Man Climbing into a Boat,* ca. 1579

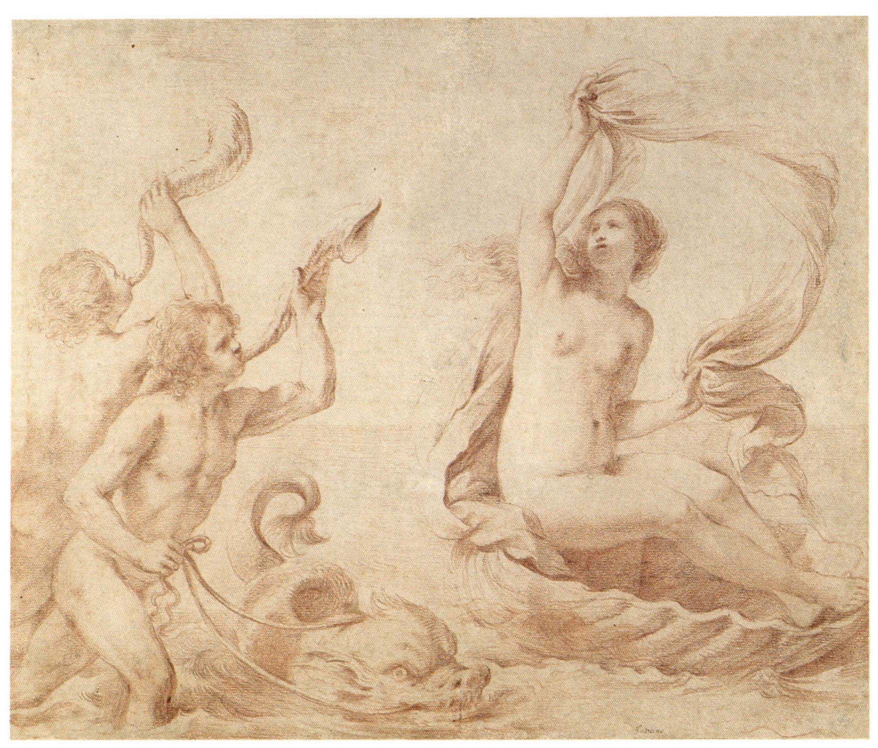

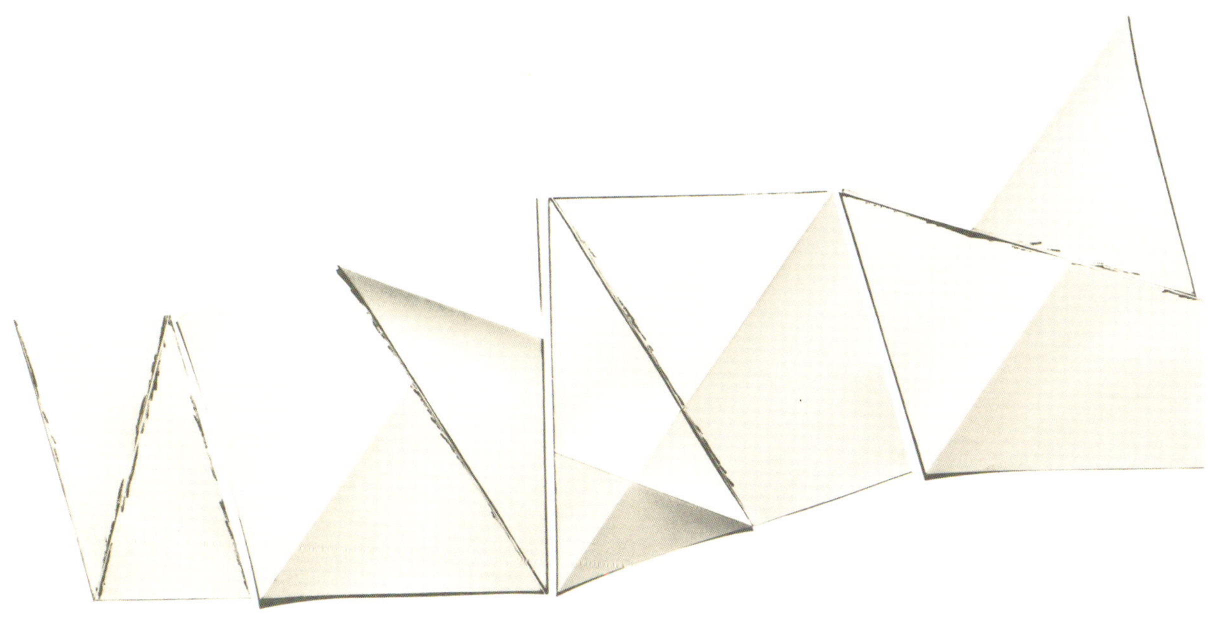

Guercino, *Galatea Accompanied by Two Tritons*, ca. 1650–60

Dorothea Rockburne, *Conservation Class #9*, 1973

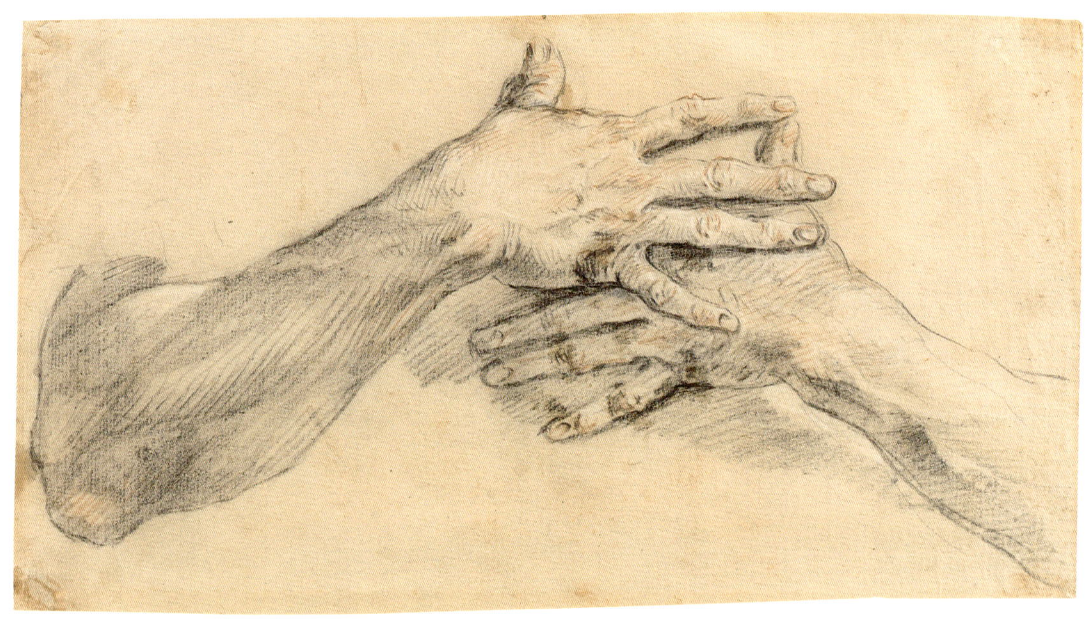

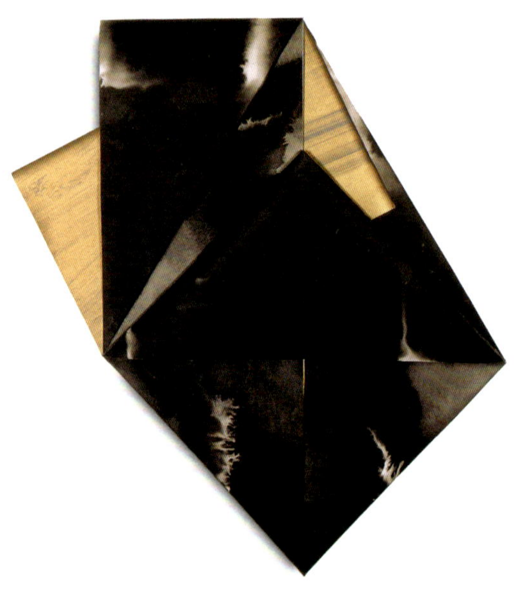

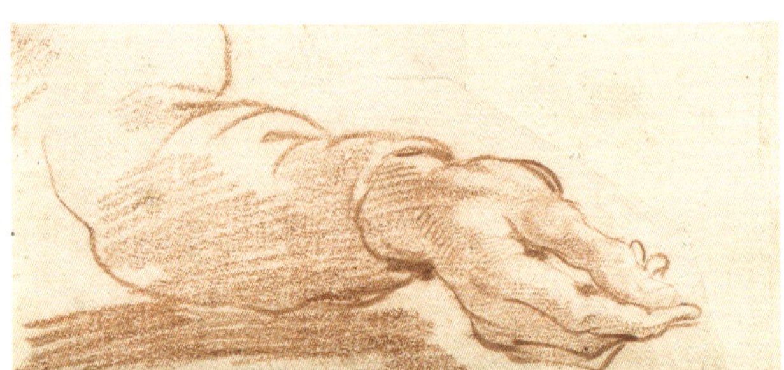

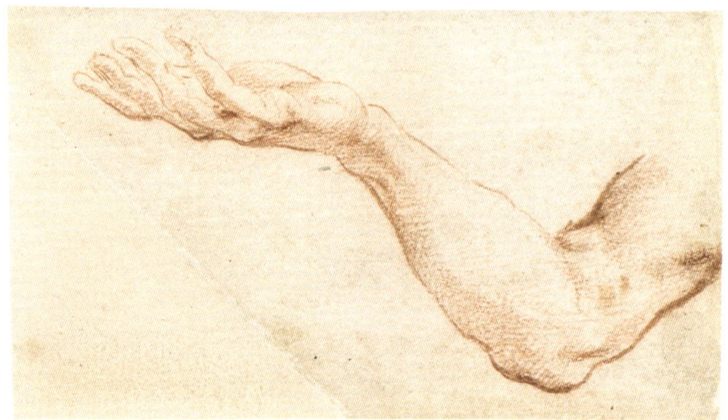

Clockwise from top:

Guido Reni, *Study of Forearms with Hands Crossed,* ca. 1613–14

Circle of Jacopo da Pontormo, *Lower Right Arm with Sleeve, Casting a Shadow*

Circle of Jacopo da Pontormo, *Right Arm and Hand, with Palm Turned Upward*

Dorothea Rockburne, *Dark Angel: Elephant,* 1982

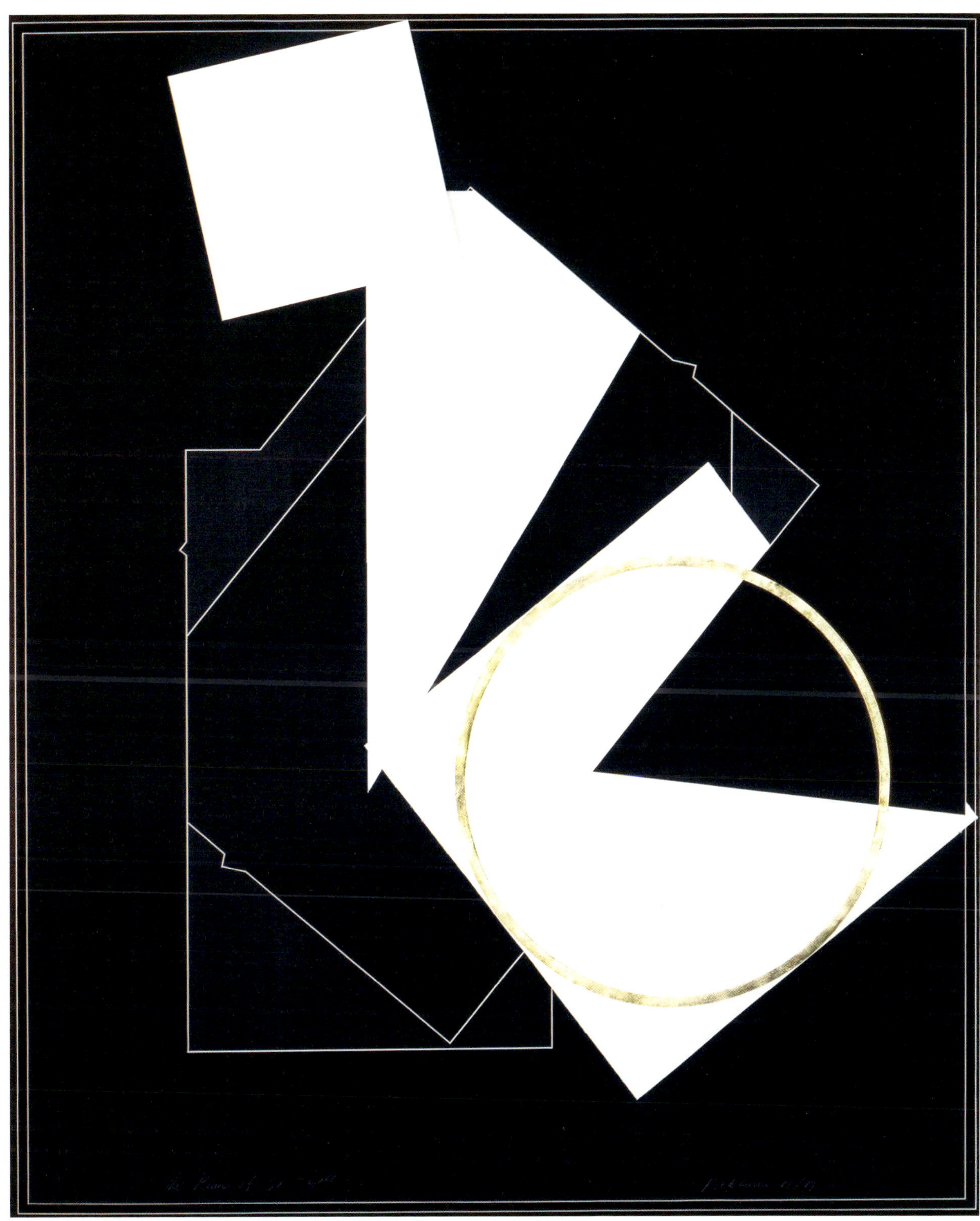

Dorothea Rockburne, *The Plan of St. Gall*, 1988–89

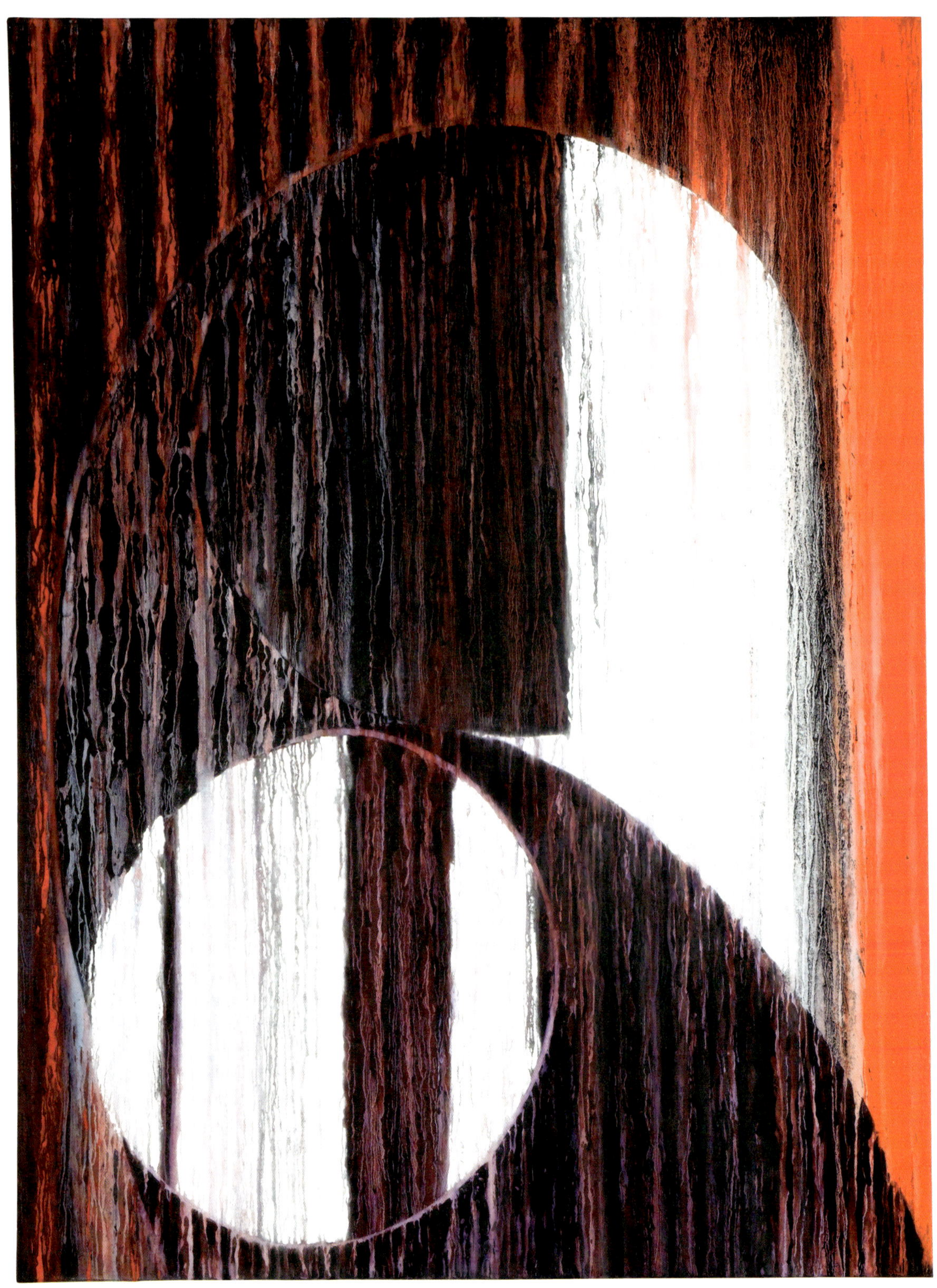

Dorothea Rockburne, *The Conjecture,* 2007

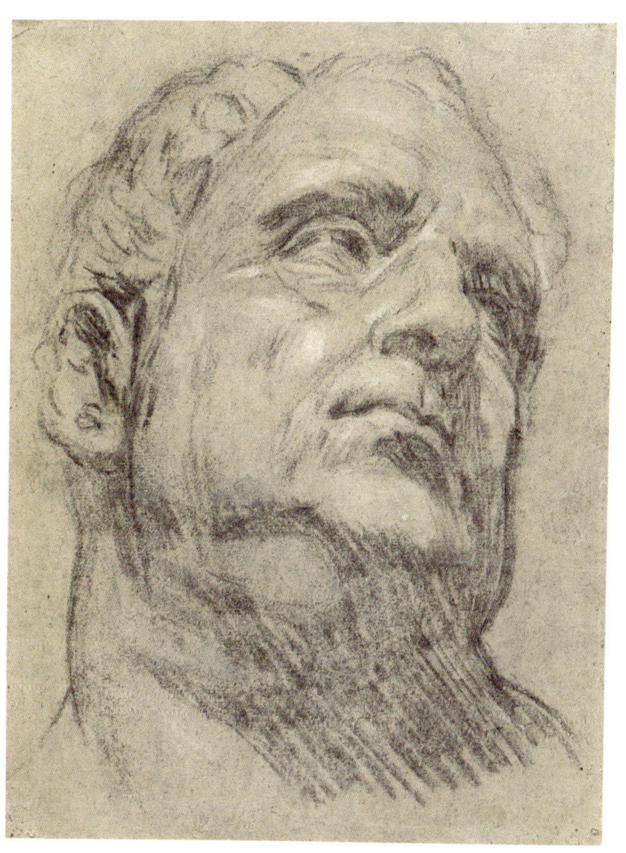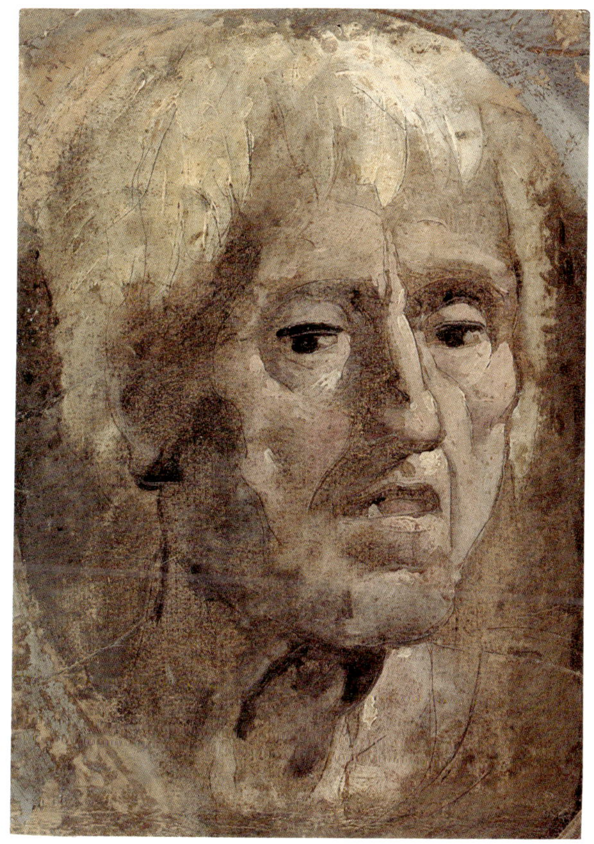

Tintoretto, So-called *Head of Emperor Vitellius*, 1540–80

Domenico Beccafumi, *Head of an Old Man with Open Mouth*, ca. 1529–35

Selected Bibliography

Albertina, Vienna, *Georg Baselitz: Die monumentalen Aquarelle/Aquarelles monumentales,* essay by Eric Darragon, 2003.

Michael Brenson, "The Artist's Eye: Dorothea Rockburne. A New-World Painter Views the Masterpieces of Old-World Innovators," *The New York Times,* 29 April 1988.

Cabinet d'art graphique, Musée national d'art moderne, Paris, *Georg Baselitz: Dessins 1962–1992,* catalogue by Fabrice Hergott, 1993.

Cabinet d'art graphique, Musée national d'art moderne, Paris, *Henri Matisse, Ellsworth Kelly: Plant Drawings,* essays by Remi Labrusse and Eric de Chassey, 2002.

Cabinet des estampes, Geneva, *Le beau style, 1520–1620: gravures maniéristes de la collection Georg Baselitz,* 2002.

Centre national d'art et de culture Georges Pompidou, Paris, *Giuseppe Penone,* catalogue by Catherine Grenier, 2004.

Chuck Close, "Dorothea Rockburne" in *The Portraits Speak: Chuck Close in Conversation with 27 of His Subjects,* New York, 1997.

David Nolan Gallery, New York, *Georg Baselitz: Watercolors,* essay by Klaus Kertess, 2007.

The Drawing Center, New York, *Giuseppe Penone: The Imprint of Drawing/L'impronta del disegno,* Catherine De Zegher, ed., 2004.

École nationale supérieure des beaux-arts, Paris, *La bella maniera: La collection d'estampes maniéristes de Georg Baselitz,* 2002.

Grand Rapids Art Museum, Michigan, *Drawn from Nature: The Plant Lithographs of Ellsworth Kelly,* catalogue by Richard H. Axsom, 2005.

Guild Hall Museum, East Hampton, New York, *Dorothea Rockburne: The Transcendent Light of Geometry,* conversation with Chuck Close and Dorothea Rockburne, 1995.

Harvard University Art Museum, Cambridge, Massachusetts, *Ellsworth Kelly: The Early Drawings 1948–1955,* catalogue by Yve-Alain Bois, 1999.

Michael Kimmelman, *Portraits: Talking with Artists at the Met, the Modern, The Louvre and Elsewhere,* New York, 1998.

Kunstmuseum Basel, *Georg Baselitz—Zeichnungen,* 1970.

Kunstmuseum Basel, *Georg Baselitz, Zeichnungen 1958–1983,* essays by Rudi H. Fuchs and Dieter Koepplin, 1984.

Lawrence Rubin-Greenberg Van Doren-Fine Art, New York, *Dorothea Rockburne: Ten Years of Astronomy Drawings 1990–2000,* conversation with Dorothea Rockburne, Rolf Sinclair, and Amy Sandback, 2000.

Matthew Marks Gallery, New York, *Ellsworth Kelly: Self-Portrait Drawings, 1944–1992,* essay by Harry Cooper, 2003.

Musée des Beaux-Arts de Nantes, *Dialogue Ininterrompu,* introduction by Guy Tosatto, 2001.

Musée du Louvre and Centre national d'art et de culture Georges Pompidou, Paris, *Comme le rêve le dessin: Dessins italiens des XVIᵉ et XVIIᵉ siècles du Musée du Louvre, Dessins contemporains du Centre Pompidou,* catalogue by Philippe-Alain Michaud, 2005.

Museum Kurhaus Kleve, *Giuseppe Penone,* essays by Guido de Werd et al., 2006–7.

National Gallery, London, *Encounters: New Art from Old,* catalogue by Richard Morphet, introduction by Robert Rosenblum, 2000.

Nyehaus, New York, *Georg Baselitz: Works from the 1960s and 1970s,* essay by Siegfried Gohr, 2006.

Giuseppe Penone, *Respirer l'ombre,* École nationale supérieure des Beaux Arts, Paris, 1999.

Pinakothek der Moderne, Munich, *Baselitz: Remix,* essays by Carla Schulz-Hoffmann and Richard Shiff, 2006.

The Southbank Centre, London, *Drawing the Line: Reappraising Drawing Past and Present. Selected by Michael Craig-Martin,* 1995.

Waldman, Diane, *Ellsworth Kelly: Drawings, Collages, Prints,* New York Graphic Society, Greenwich, Conn., 1971.